The Magnificent Mesquite

NUMBER FORTY-SIX

THE CORRIE HERRING HOOKS SERIES

The majestic, wide-spreading National Champion mesquite is located near Leakey, Texas. (Photo © Mark Duff, Kerrville, Texas)

The Magnificent Mesquite

KEN E. ROGERS

UNIVERSITY OF TEXAS PRESS
AUSTIN

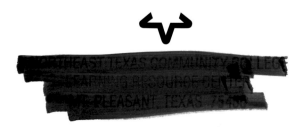

[redacted]

Excerpt from *The Legumes of Texas* by B. L. Turner reprinted by permission of the University of Texas Press.

"The Old Mesquites Ain't Out" by Frank Grimes, © *Abilene Reporter-News*, December 9, 1931, reprinted by permission.

Efforts to trace the copyright holder for "Where Longhorn Bones Lie Bleached" by Faye Carr Adams, "Mesquite" by Faye Carr Adams, and "Mesquite" by Boyce House have been unsuccessful.

Printed in Hong Kong By C & C Offset Printing Co., Ltd.

First edition, 2000

∞ The paper used in this book meets the minimum requirements of ANSI/NISO Z39.48-1992 (R1997) (Permanence of Paper).

LIBRARY OF CONGRESS
CATALOGING-IN-PUBLICATION DATA

Rogers, Ken E.
The magnificent mesquite / Ken E. Rogers.— 1st ed.
p. cm. — (The Corrie Herring Hooks series ; no. 46)
Includes bibliographical reference and index.
ISBN 0-292-77105-3 (hardcover : alk. paper)
1. Mesquite. I.Title. II. Series
SB317.M47 R64 2000
634.9'73748—DC21
99-050890

Design by J. Clemente Orozco

To my bride, Kathy—thanks for putting up with me for all these years . . .

A Kathy, para siempre, con amor sempiterno.

To Kendall and Kourtney, my two special kids, to whom nothing on earth can compare. Always remember to believe in yourself and stay true to yourself; and always remember the words of the Master: all things are possible to those who believe.

To the best mother in the world, who gave me the thirst for lifelong learning and who has known how to love others, serve others, and give and give and give . . . there is a special crown with the most valuable of jewels made just for you.

To my friend Roy Willmon, who took me under his wing and befriended me many years ago when I was searching, I give my sincere thanks—and remember always, there is a great day coming.

To my dear friends Jean and Rogers Craig, real pioneers in the mesquite business. You are true Amigos del Mesquite.

And finally to Dewayne Weldon, who has shown me for over twenty-five years how to live in this world and how to forgive in this world: I thank you from the bottom of my heart. Viva Vieques!

Contents

Introduction

Over the past several centuries, probably no one plant has played a greater and more vital role in the lives of humankind in the southwestern United States than the short, crooked mesquite. Relying on mesquite for a myriad of necessities such as food, weapons, shelter, and medicine, early southwestern Indians drew upon it in almost every aspect of their lives, even giving it a position of honor in their religious ceremonies. During times of drought and pestilence mesquite supplied early western travelers and settlers with both food and shelter for survival, as almost all parts of the tree were used. The mesquite that dominated the dense brush on millions of acres of the southwestern United States conveyed many emotions to humans, who looked at it as a noble warrior, confronted it as a powerful adversary, or were drawn to it for survival. Many, like the great southwestern author and folklorist J. Frank Dobie, had a deep reverence for the mesquite, as seen in his 1941 *Arizona Highways* article:

> As a tree, mesquite seems to me as graceful and lovely as any tree in the world. When, in the spring, trees and bushes put on their delicately green, transparent leaves and the mild sun shines upon them, they are more beautiful than any peach orchard. The green seems to float through the young sunlight into the sky. The mesquite is itself a poem.
>
> Primroses burn their yellow fires
> Where grass and roadway meet;
> Feathered and tasseled like a queen,
> Is every old mesquite. . . .
>
> . . . It comes as near characteristic of the whole Southwest including much of Mexico, as any species of plant life known to the region. It is as native as rattlesnakes and mocking birds, as characteristic as northers, and as blended into the life of the land as cornbread and tortillas. Men and other animals were using it untold generations before Columbus sailed; they are still making use of it.

Mesquite was part of the nature of the Southwest, of its undaunted people and its awesome history, with a tenacious temperament that has both supported humans and hindered their interests. It has become an icon for the Southwest (especially for Texas): an image and symbol of the harshness of its environment, the toughness of its native people, and the perseverance of the early westward settlers who looked over the next ridge to a new challenge. Dobie makes the compelling statement that lovers of the mesquite through the years might have made: "For me it is emblematic like the Lone Star and a pair of horns of a Longhorn steer. I ask for no better monument over my grave than a good mesquite tree" (*Dallas Morning News*, February 9, 1941, 12).

Mesquite's doubly compound leaves and spike flowers are very showy in the spring and summer months. (Photo © Ken E. Rogers)

People of many cultures through the years have considered mesquite an indispensable resource. Mesquite was important to the early Indians for both subsistence and aesthetic purposes; they used this most valuable of friends for the construction of shelters and for day-to-day items such as weapons, medicines, recreational paraphernalia, ointments, and implements for farming and food preparation. Early settlers and ranchers trying to scratch out an existence on the trying lands both praised mesquite and swore at it with the most degrading words. During extreme droughts and severe winters, mesquite provided omnipresent food; ranchers heaped praise on this worthy partner for supplying precious food and cooling shade for drought-starved livestock.

Mesquite beans are a favorite food of many domestic and wild animals. (Photo © Ken E. Rogers)

But they also cussed it and spit at it through the years for its terrible thorniness and its aggressive invasion of beloved grasslands, sapping precious soil moisture. People have never truly understood this magnificent tree and its role in the historical events of the Southwest.

Many travelers crossing the plains of the Southwest survived on the mesquite bean. When the 320-man Texas–Santa Fe Expedition sent by the Republic of Texas to annex New Mexico crossed the Texas Panhandle in the summer of 1841, they found the mesquite bean and called it "manna from heaven." "When our provisions and coffee ran out," wrote George W. Kendall (1844), a New Orleans journalist who joined the expedition, "the men ate them in immense quantities, and roasted or boiled them!"

Due to their availability and durability, mesquite timbers were used in the construction of Fort Richardson in 1867 near Jacksboro (originally called Mesquiteville), Texas, the northernmost of a line of federal forts established after the Civil War and home of Colonel Ranald Mackenzie's Fourth Cavalry. Mesquite wood's reputation for resistance to decay and insect attack was well known.

The earliest North American botanical account of mesquite, also widely known by its genus name *Prosopis*, was published in 1788 by the Swedish traveler Peter Olof Swartz. He found a species of the genus *Prosopis* that had naturalized itself in Jamaica in the Caribbean and originally classified it as a mimosa, *Mimosa juliflora*. The tree was first found and identified as *Prosopis* within the territory of the United States in the valley of the Canadian River near the northern limits of its distribution in 1820 by Dr. Edwin P. James, the naturalist of Major Stephen Long's Rocky Mountain Expedition.

In 1828 Stephen F. Austin, who was to become the "Father of Texas," declared that Texas was "as desirable a country for all the wants and necessities of man as any other on earth." His description, intended for a pamphlet circulated in Europe, praised the qualities of a "low tree called Muskite": "The tree is highly valued and afforded excellent firewood and valuable material for fencing" (Wright 1965, 38).

Another Southwest mesquite, screwbean mesquite (*Prosopis pubescens*), or tornillo as the Mexicans call it, was discovered by John Charles Frémont, a soldier, explorer, and politician, most famous as the "pathmaker of the West" due to his mapmaking skills in the Mohave Desert in 1843 during his second transcontinental journey.

Impressions of this marvelous tree of the prairie were recorded by many pioneer travelers. Almost without exception, they saw mesquite's open, spreading form as resembling the peach tree. Fifty miles from the Guadalupe River, in DeWitt's Colony on a trip to San Antonio, J. C. Clopper wrote in his "Journal and Book of Memoranda for 1828": " . . . when we enter upon what is here called musquite prairie . . . The trunk and growth of the branches are more after the form and appearance of a peach—and indeed at a distance the whole prairies or country seems like an immense peach orchard . . ." (Clopper 1828, 69). After spending the winter in San Antonio in 1872, poet Sidney Lanier in his essay "The Texas Trail in the 70's" described a trip made in the New Braunfels area:

> Presently I observed the stage-lamps continually light up a curious sort of bare struggling-twigged shrub that seems to line the road and to cover the prairie. It is as if the apparitions of all the leafless-peach-orchards in Georgia were lawlessly dancing past us and about us. (Lanier 1913, 583)

Many other early travelers also compared the spread of the mesquite to the beautiful peach, and to this day people look at the mesquite and comment on its closeness to the peach tree in upward spreading form and profile.

The common name "mesquite," as we know it today, has gone through many changes. According to *Webster's New International Dictionary* (1961), the word "mesquite" may be pronounced either *mĕs´-kēt* or *mĕs-kēt´*. The word comes from the Uto-Aztecan Nahuatl word for the tree, *misquitl*. In the spelling of the common name, many authors have followed botanist John M. Coulter, a member of the Lewis and Clark expedition, in adopting the Spanish *mezquite*, as did frontiersman Josiah Gregg in his 1844 two-volume *Commerce of the Prairies*, a compilation which includes writings about his travels through Texas and up the Red River valley. James Ohio Pattie, who in 1826 become one of the first Americans to explore the Grand Canyon, called it "musqueto" wood in his 1831 book *The Personal Narrative of James O. Pattie of Kentucky during an Expedition from St. Louis, through the Vast Regions between That Place and the Pacific Ocean*. In volume five of the 1927 book *Papers of Mirabeau Buonaparte Lamar*, editor, historian, and early Texas State Library archivist Harriet Wingfield Smither calls it "muscet." William McClintock, in his "Journal of a Trip through Texas and Northern Mexico in 1846–1847," published in the *Southwestern Historical Quarterly* in 1930, calls it "musquit," as does historian Henderson K. Yoakum in his well-known 1855 two-volume *History of Texas from Its First Settlement in 1685 to Its Annexation to the United States in 1846.* George W. Kendall in 1844, in his *Narrative of the Texas Santa Fe Expedition,* is given credit for first using our modern-day spelling.

Mesquite has also been given many names throughout the years by different cultures. Each early American Indian tribe gave it their own name. The Seri and Papago Indians who lived in mesquite country used the terms *das* and *kui*, respectively. Today mesquite goes by many common names used extensively worldwide. In North America most species are usually simply called mesquite or honey mesquite after the most common species in the United States, *Prosopis glandulosa.* Among Spanish-speaking people of the Southwest the fruit of the mesquite is known as la péchita, derived from the Opata word *péchit*, meaning mesquite fruit. In South America it is routinely called algarrobo, venal, or chamacoco; in the Middle East jand, ghaf, or acatin; in India khejri; and in Hawaii kiawe. Worldwide, many local names exist in many languages.

Mesquite's Common Names

Mesquite goes by many common names worldwide. I use the most popular common name when discussing mesquite's presence and role in a particular region. In the southwestern United States and in Mexico "mesquite" and "mezquite" (common in Mexico) are generally used. In Argentina and much of South America mesquite is refered to either as algarrobo or by its genus, *Prosopis*. In India and Hawaii it is referred to as khejri and kiawe, respectively. Worldwide, almost everyone will understand which tree you are refering to if you call it *Prosopis*. A complete list of *Prosopis* species, locations, and common names can be found in Appendix 1.

Perhaps the first Spaniard to chronicle the Indians' use of mesquite was explorer Alvar Núñez Cabeza de Vaca of Pánfilo de Narváez's Florida expedition of 1528; with three companions, Alonso del Castillo Maldonado, Andrés Dorantes, and the African slave Estevan, he wandered captive for much of the period from 1528 to 1536, traveling along the Texas Gulf Coast and across Texas with Southwest Indian tribes. After being shipwrecked on the Texas coast, Cabeza de Vaca approached the Rio Grande and observed the Indians preparing a mesquitamal flour from the "mezquiquez."

> After parting with those we left weeping, we went with the others to their houses and were hospitably received by the people in them. They brought their children to us that we might touch their hands, and gave us a great quantity of the flour of mezquiquez. The fruit while hanging on the tree, is very bitter and like unto the carob; when eaten with earth it is sweet and wholesome. The method they have of preparing it is this? They make a hole of requisite depth in the ground, and throwing in the fruit, pound it with a club the size of a leg, a fathom and a half in length, until it is well mashed. Besides the earth that comes from the hole, they bring and add some handfulls, then returning to beat it a little while longer. Afterward it is thrown into a jar, like a basket, upon which water is poured until it rises above and covers the mixture. He that beats it tastes it, and if it appears to him not sweet, he asks for earth to stir in, which is added until he finds it sweet. Then all sit round, and each putting in a hand, takes out as much as he can. The pits and hulls are thrown upon a skin, whence they are taken by him who does the pounding, and put into the jar whereon water is poured as at first, whence having expressed the froth and juice, again the pits and husks are thrown upon the skin. This they do three or four times to each pounding. Those present, for whom this is a great banquet, have their stomachs greatly distended by the earth and water they swallow. The Indians made a protracted festival of this sort on our account, and great areitos during the time we remained. (Smith 1871, 140–141)

Large quantities of mesquite beans were used by the Coahuiltecan Indians, who were called the Acubados or Arbadaos by Cabeza de Vaca. In one of their feasts after victories in feuds with other tribes, one of the unusual and grotesque mystical ceremonial practices was to eat mesquitamal flour mixed with the pulverized bones of fellow warriors who had died of natural causes.

In the early and mid-1800s mesquite wood was a favorite of craftspersons in the design of Early Texas style furniture. Its durability, stability, and availability proved attractive to these artists crafting furniture in styles adopted from the eastern culture. Mesquite was used as street paving blocks in Alamo Plaza and on other downtown streets in San Antonio by laying down a layer of sand and a surface layer of eight- to twelve-inch hexagonal mesquite blocks, making the streets passable during rainy weather. These blocks remained the road surface of choice until the discovery of the Texas oil reserves, after which asphalt tar was placed on the mesquite blocks to even out the surface. To this day, when the streets of San Antonio are excavated, mesquite blocks can still be found as the undersurface on many streets.

In the 1800s and early 1900s streets of many cities such as San Antonio were paved with mesquite blocks to make them passable during rainy seasons.

Today many craftspersons are making beautiful desks, chairs, floors, wall panels, and mantles from mesquite wood. Due to the ease of drying and working the wood and its extremely low shrinkage rate, mesquite has become a favorite of craftspersons worldwide for novelties, wood turnings, and sculptures. Working with mesquite gives the craftsperson a feeling that the wood is participating in the creation of the art.

According to the overwhelming majority of woodworkers who have had the great opportunity to have crafted items from mesquite, it is one of the world's finest woods for furniture and flooring. Its mechanical and physical properties give exceptional performance and beauty. Mesquite's deep, rich colors, when mixed with its natural graininess and character markings, result in a fine floor, seldom matched. Mesquite wood is exceptionally hard—nearly twice as hard as oak and wal-

Current Uses of Mesquite
in the Southwestern United States

- Fine solid wood products
- Carvings, turnings, sculptures, flooring, jewelry, boxes, paneling, veneers, pens/pencils, clocks, humidors, lumber, fireplace mantles, rocking chairs, tables, doors, desks, other furniture.
- Ornamental landscape specimens
- Firewood and stovewood
- Fenceposts
- Cooking and smoking wood
- Chips, chunks, flakes, mini-logs, compressed chip-logs, sawdust
- Foods and flavorings
- Liquid smoke, jellies, honey, pod flour
- Livestock fodder and shade
- Wildlife habitat food, cooling shade and cover (deer, turkey, quail, dove, etc.)

nut; and its dimensional stability (its stability when exposed to extreme moisture situations)—a property prized in the furniture and flooring industries—is about four times that of competing woods.

Mesquite lumber is mainly produced at small, often portable sawmills. Twenty or more mills operate in Texas, with many others in New Mexico and Arizona and an extensive mesquite sawmilling industry in Argentina and Mexico. The vast majority of mesquite trees commercially harvested are used in the cooking and smoking of meats. Barbecuing has become a very attractive way of preparing foods, and mesquite has become the wood of choice; more than 100,000 cords of mesquite are harvested annually to be sold in the barbecue wood and firewood industries. After being processed into chunks, chips, slivers, charcoal, liquid smoke, and sawdust, the wood is packaged and sent to retail markets throughout the United States and worldwide.

Mesquite trees produce a type of gum that was highly sought after as an alternative to gum arabic in the early 1900s. A report of the United States Dispensatory in 1872 stated that about 24,000 pounds of mesquite gum was gathered in Texas. The gum was shipped to the East to confectioners, who used it to make gumdrops. Little if any mesquite gum is harvested and used now.

Today one of the mesquite's most widespread uses is as a nectar source for bees. Mesquite is a very reliable bloomer, earning it praise from honey producers. Many *Prosopis* species are known to be excellent bee forage. Mesquite honey has a very delicate, mild flavor in great demand in the commercial honey industry. Mesquite is considered the most valuable honey plant in Arizona, Texas, Hawaii, and many locations worldwide.

The center of diversity of *Prosopis* is in Argentina, where scientists have concluded the genus originated. Thirty-four of the known forty-four *Prosopis* species are found on the South American continent. A list of *Prosopis* species and their geographical range can be found in Appendix 1.

Mesquite grows naturally in North America in the arid and semi-arid lands of the Southwest, primarily in Texas, Oklahoma, Arizona, and New Mexico, where it inhabits more than 82 million acres. It also grows in limited ranges in California, Colorado, Utah, Nevada, and Kansas. Records of the earliest travelers and settlers suggest that mesquite has not substantially increased its geographical range in the south-

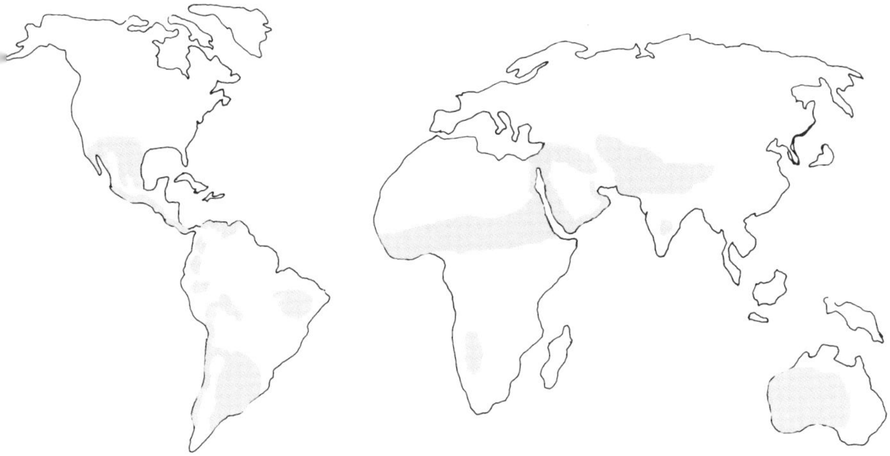

Mesquite's general geographical distribution in the world.
(Developed from Burkart 1976, Johnson and Mayeux 1990, Simpson 1977, Turner 1959, Vines 1976, and other sources)

western United States, but it has greatly increased its density within that range. In the early 1800s miles and miles of grasslands existed in the Southwest, characterized by extensive grassy plains, moderate grass-mesquite savannas, and dense mesquite mottes (clumps of isolated trees) in and around creeks and small bodies of water. Francis Francis (1887) described the Texas rangeland as "wave after wave of rolling country sparsely covered with mesquitis bush." Many of those same rangeland sites are now totally infested with mesquite. Investigators have concluded that this rapid invasion of mesquite occurred primarily due to three catalysts: the overgrazing of fenced grasslands by domestic cattle, the control and elimination of wildfires, and several recorded periodic droughts during the early 1900s.

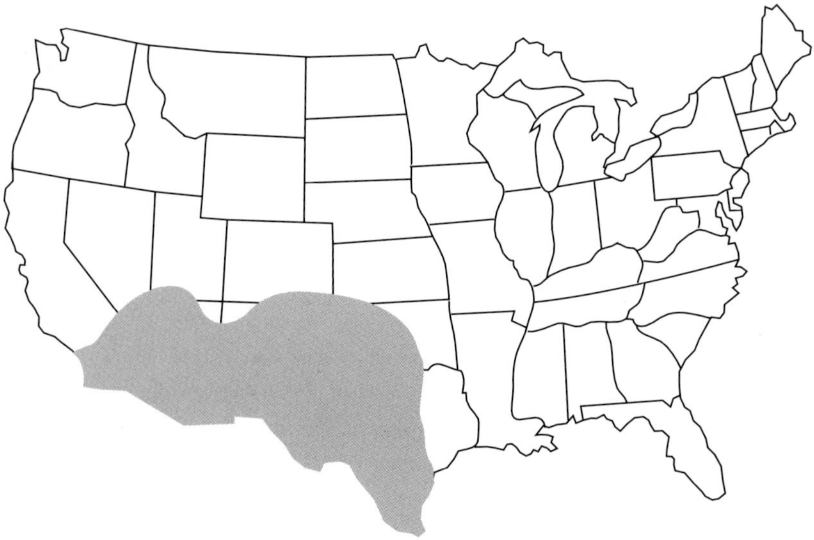

Mesquite's general geographical distribution in Texas and the southwestern United States. (Developed from Burkart 1976, Johnson and Mayeux 1990, Simpson 1977, Turner 1959, Vines 1976, and other sources)

In contrast to all of the benefits that mesquite has supplied to many diverse cultures for hundreds of years, since the late 1800s it has been considered a pest on the rangelands of the southwestern United States and in many other regions worldwide. Mesquite is one of the most damaging plants of these rangelands; estimates made in 1985 of the losses caused by mesquite in the livestock industry alone were 200 to 500 million dollars annually, primarily because it competes with native grasses for limited soil moisture. On lands that mesquite has taken over, critical losses of soil moisture have driven out many native plants and grasses, leaving a dense, unusable stand of mesquite.

Worldwide, five species of mesquite are uniquely aggressive weeds that cause devastation to native grasslands: honey mesquite (*Prosopis glandulosa*), native to the southwestern United States and northern Mexico; venal (*Prosopis ruscifolia*) and algarrobo (*Prosopis nigra*), native to Bolivia, Paraguay, and Argentina; algarrobo or algarrobo dulce (*Prosopis flexuosa*), native to Argentina; and algarrobo (*Prosopis juliflora*), native to Central America, northern South America, and the West

Indies. These five species, unlike most other *Prosopis* species and unlike their competitive range grasses, invade and spread rapidly due to their ease of propagation and their ability to withstand adverse conditions such as drought and poor growing sites.

Control by hand grubbing and chopping out the invading mesquites and by mechanical methods using tractors and dozers has become far too expensive except in unique situations. Chemical control has been only marginally effective and successful. Both mechanical and chemical methods are used extensively in the southwestern United States, hardly maintaining a status quo with mesquite's aggressive spread. The best management tool for mesquite on rangeland may be the use of prescribed fires. Fire is especially beneficial when used in a management regime that combines it with mechanical or chemical control techniques.

Mesquite was introduced and subsequently escaped cultivation in Australia, the Philippines, the Sudan, and Hawaii. Projected to be an "erosion control savior," mesquite has become a great pest in these regions of the world, invading, competing, and overwhelming both native grasses and other woody plants. In some locations mesquite has actually become a much greater problem than the previously existing arid conditions.

Yet despite, or because of, its reputation as an aggressive invader, mesquite is being utilized extensively worldwide to combat desertification, the gradual conversion of drylands to nonproductive lands. Desertification is caused by many factors, such as extended drought, excessive land cropping, overgrazing, overcultivation, and the mismanagement of irrigated croplands. Many species of mesquite are ideal for this use, because they require less than four inches of rainfall annually to establish themselves and survive. In India, China, Peru, Chile, Pakistan, and many African nations, mesquite not only provides a barrier to desertification, but also serves as a multipurpose tree, providing fodder for livestock, pods for human consumption, and fuelwood for heating and cooking. A windbreak of mesquite trees two miles wide and four hundred miles long is being planted in India to encounter wind erosion caused by careless farming that is causing the Rajputana (Thar) desert to advance eastward toward New Delhi.

Research into mesquite ecosystem management is ongoing throughout the world. The current thought of many researchers and range managers is that mesquite can be of great value to livestock and to wildlife because it supplies forage, cover, and cooling shade and increases the fertility of the soil through nitrogen fixation and its contribution of organic matter. Mesquite's role cannot be overemphasized, as many of these drier sites where the mesquite is present have very infertile soils with low levels of organic matter and nitrogen. The ideal situation is to have a well-managed savanna-type range with an occasional mesquite to provide shade and cover, with the trees managed for infrequent wood product harvest for cooking, furniture, flooring, and other fine wood uses.

As society begins a new millennium, mesquite will become a more important resource for humankind by playing a more positive role in the health and productivity of the rangeland ecosystem. Society has the responsibility to understand the role of mesquite and its interaction with other elements of the ecosystem and has the opportunity to assist mesquite in making a major contribution to its ecosystem and, in turn, to humankind.

Mesquite: What Is It?

Mesquite (*Prosopis* spp.) is a perennial belonging to the Mimosoideae subfamily of the Leguminosae/Fabaceae. Like nearly all Leguminosae/ Fabaceae, mesquite trees produce their seeds in legumes or pods. Members of the Mimosoideae subfamily are distinguished from other legumes by three characteristics: small flowers clustered into an inflorescence (an axis along which all the buds are flower buds), pinnately (or doubly) compound leaves with stipules (leaflike appendages at the base of the petiole of the leaves), and regular flowers with a five-part corolla (the inner circle of flower leaves or petals). Anywhere in the world, *Prosopis* can be distinguished from other members of the Mimosoideae subfamily in that *Prosopis* species have fleshy pods that do not open to release the seeds when they are mature (this is called indehiscence) and their pollen is released as single grains.

Carolus Linnaeus, professor of natural history at the University of Uppsala, Stockholm, and originator of the binomial system for naming plants and animals, who in his lifetime named more than nine thousand plants, selected the name *Prosopis* in 1767 in his book *Mantissa Plantarum* for the genus classified by only one species he had seen, *Prosopis spicigera*, which grows in the Near East. *Prosopis*, derived from ancient Greek, means a kind of prickly fruit. The second species was *Prosopis chilensis*, described by Chilean botanist Ignacio Molina in 1782, originally called *Ceratonia chilensis*. Peter Olof Swartz, curator of the botanical collections at the Royal Swedish Academy of Sciences in Stockholm, classified the third species in 1788 as *Mimosa juliflora* and reclassified it as *Prosopis juliflora* in 1825. Since the early 1800s, there have been many additions, deletions, and changes in the classification scheme of the genus *Prosopis*. *Prosopis* species have been placed in many genera, including *Acacia*, *Spirolobium*, *Strombocarpa*, *Mimosa*, *Neltuma*, and *Ceratonia*. It was not until 1976, with the completion of a worldwide classification by Arturo Burkart, that the genus *Prosopis* was generally accepted for all forty-four species worldwide.

Prosopis exhibits tremendous variance in growth forms and plant characteristics, ranging from tree size (forty to fifty feet tall) to very small, prostrate, vinelike forms. Widely expanding in its tree canopy, mesquite is often multistemmed, branching at or close to the ground. Leaves of the various mesquite species range from the foot-long, pin-

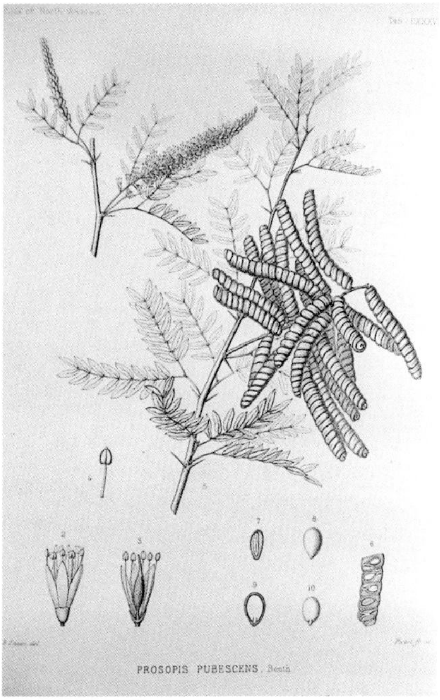

Prosopis pubescens
Plate 138 by Charles Edward Faxon, artist, taken from Charles Sprague Sargent's *The Silva of North America* (1891).
(Photo © Ken E. Rogers)

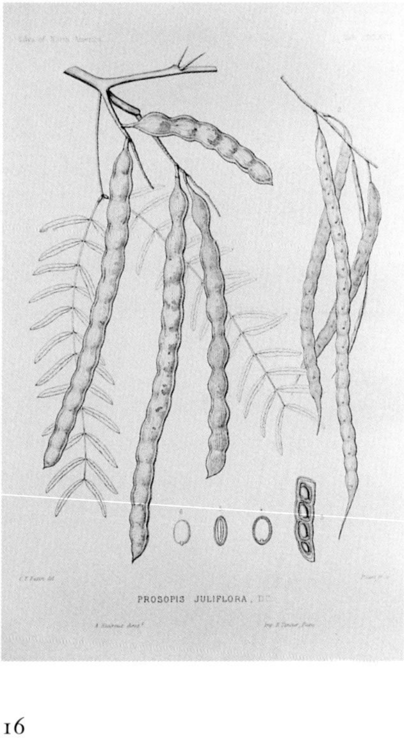

Prosopis juliflora
Plate 137 by Charles Edward Faxon, artist, taken from Charles Sprague Sargent's *The Silva of North America* (1891).
(Photo © Ken E. Rogers)

A Classification System for the Plant Kingdom

A classification system governed by an internationally accepted Code of Botanical Nomenclature has been developed, which divides the plant kingdom into progressively smaller groups: division, class, order, family, genus, and species. Intermediate categories are often formed by adding the prefix "sub" to the preceding terms (for example, subfamily, subgenus, and subspecies); by further dividing a genus into sections and series; or by dividing a species into varieties and forms.

A family is a group of genera whose members resemble one another in several respects. A genus is made up of more closely related and similar plant species. Sections and series are further subdivisions of a genus, dividing it into categories with one or more distinctive characteristics. Plants of a species are similar in a number of characteristics and are normally interfertile and breed true. A variety differs from others of the same species in one or a few characteristics. For example, the flowers may be different in color or the leaves different in shape. A form denotes minor genetic variants that sporadically occur in populations, such as an occasional change in flower color.

All plants have a binomial (two-part) name consisting of the genus name followed by the specific epithet. Together these two parts make up the species name for a plant. For example, in the case of *Prosopis glandulosa* var. *glandulosa*, *Prosopis* is the genus, *glandulosa* is the specific epithet, *glandulosa* is also the variety, and *Prosopis glandulosa* is the name of the species.

nately compound, lacy, fernlike leaves of most species, giving a delicate look, to the extremely small leaves of the species *Prosopis kuntzei*, which essentially lacks leaves for most of the year, appearing to bear only thorns. Most *Prosopis* species have thorns, solitary or in pairs, that protrude sharply from the stem. The flowers of some species are long, yellow spikes, whereas others are round, reddish balls. Mesquite beans also exhibit extreme diversity in form: the pods of some species are large, flat, fleshy, and light green; the pods of others are long and tightly coiled or corkscrewed or short, dry, and almost totally black.

The forty-four species of *Prosopis* are distributed in arid and semiarid areas of North and South America; in India, Pakistan, the Philippines, and the Middle East in Asia; in South and North Africa; and in Australia. Only three species exist naturally in Asia; and one additional species is native to Africa. Forty of the forty-four species are New World natives, with North America being the native home of nine species. Thirty-one species are native to South America. Although mesquite has infested thousands of acres of rangeland in Australia, it is not native there; mesquite was introduced on a widespread basis in programs to combat soil erosion and to stop desertification or as livestock fodder.

Mesquite Biology and Growth

Mesquite is very adaptive to a wide range of soil types under a wide range of moisture conditions. Its adaptability to adverse conditions was noticed even back in the nineteenth century: Victor Havard, writing in the *American Naturalist* in 1884, commented on the mesquite's innate ability to survive:

> . . . there is hardly any soil, if it is not habitually damp, in which mesquite cannot grow; no hill too rocky or broken, no flat too sandy or saline, no dune too shifting, no prairie too often burned, to entirely exclude it. (Havard 1884, 455)

Mesquite has its most difficult time establishing itself on sites with high soil moisture and those that have extremely deep sandy topsoil without lower clay sublayers. A plant of arid and semiarid environ-

Table 1. The Natural Geographical Areas of Development of the Species of Prosopis

AREA	NUMBER OF SPECIES	SPECIES
Southwest Asia, North Africa	3	*P. cineraria*, *P. farcta* var. *farcta*, var. *glabra*, *P. koelziana*
Tropical Africa	1	*P. africana*
Texas-Mexico	9	*P. pubescens*,* *P. palmeri*, *P. articulata*,* *P. tamaulipana*, *P. laevigata*,* *P. juliflora*, *P. glandulosa*,* *P. velutina*,* *P. reptans* var. *cinerascens**
Tropical Andean Region (Colombia to extreme northern Chile and northwestern Argentina)	6	*P. ferox*, *P. tamarugo*, *P. burkartii*, *P. pallida*, *P. chilensis*, *P. juliflora*
Argentinian Paraguayan Center and Neighboring Areas	23	*P. humilis*, *P. rojasiana*, *P. strombulifera*, *P. sericantha*, *P. kuntzei*, *P. reptans*, *P. abbreviata*, *P. torquata*, *P. ruscifolia*, *P. fiebrigii*, *P. vinalillo*, *P. hassleri*, *P. rubriflora*, *P. campestris*, *P. affinis*, *P. elata*, *P. chilensis*, *P. nigra*, *P. caldenia*, *P. flexuosa*, *P. alpataco*, *P. alba*, *P. pugionata*
Patagonion and Cuyo Region	5	*P. argentina*, *P. denudans*, *P. ruizleali*, *P. castellanosii*, *P. calingastana*

Source: Developed from Burkart 1976.

* Indicates species found in Texas [redacted]

Table 2. The Species of Prosopis *Introduced into Areas of the World*

AREA	NUMBER OF SPECIES	SPECIES
Asia	3	*P. glandulosa* (southern Arabia, Pakistan, India, Burma), *P. juliflora* (Iraq, Pakistan, India, Vietnam), *P. pallida* (India)
Tropical Africa	1	*P. juliflora* var. *juliflora* (Senegal)
South and Southwest Africa	3	*P. pubescens*, *P. chilensis* var. *catamarcana*, *P. glandulosa*
Pacific Islands (Hawaii, Marquesas, and Philippines)	2	*P. pallida* formae *pallida* and *armata*, *P. juliflora*
Australia	5	*P. pallida*, *P. chilensis*, *P. juliflora* (Queensland), *P. glandulosa*, *P. velutina*
Antilles (West Indian Islands, Cuba, Hispaniola, Jamaica, Puerto Rico)	3	*P. pallida*, *P. juliflora*, *P. glandulosa*
Brazil	1	*P. juliflora*

Source: Developed from Burkart 1976.

ments, mesquite has adapted itself to warm subtropical and tropical climates. The species of mesquite in the United States establish themselves and grow best on elevations less than 4,500 feet. Temperature seems to control mesquite's northernmost extent in the United States: its northern limit appears to follow the average minimum temperature isotherm of -3° F. Worldwide, mesquite's ability to withstand low temperatures varies greatly among species, but it generally is best adapted to areas with 200 or more frost-free days annually. Mesquite's eastern and western limits in the United States may be controlled by a combination of high soil moisture and low soil oxygen. Many scientists have also concluded that another controlling factor that limits mesquite's range is high soil acidity (low soil pH), which prevents mesquite's growth.

Over its lifetime, a mesquite tree grows through three distinct stages. Initially, in the seed/seedling stage, it is very tender and extremely prone to damage by predators, drought, fire, and weather conditions, causing a high mortality rate. Mesquite seeds are normally brown, oval, and about the size of a pea, contained in a legume pod, with a bony protective covering around each seed. For seed germination to initiate, this tough covering must be broken by some agent. Two natural agents commonly break this barrier: weather and animals. Mesquite seeds usually stay dormant, often for years, lying on the ground until their seed coat is broken by the absorption of water during inclement weather. The seed coat is also commonly broken by exposure to the acids in the digestive system of various livestock and wild animals. Research has shown that more than 50 percent of mesquite seeds that pass through horse and cattle digestive systems germinate.

Mid-1800s cattle drive trails such as the Shawnee Trail (originating in Brownsville, Texas, passing through Oklahoma, and ending in the most westward railhead in St. Louis, Missouri) and the Goodnight Trail (originating in Belknap, Texas, going through Fort Sumner, New Mexico, and terminating in Granada, Colorado) can be identified from the large increase in mesquite growth along their path. Cattle in their trek northward would eat the sweet, nutritious mesquite pods, carry them in their stomach for a few miles, and then deposit them on the trail. These were ideal conditions for seed germination, as the acids in the digestive process stratified the seedcoat and the cattle deposited the seed on the trail in a bed of moist, fertile manure.

After the germination process begins, water uptake from the soil is rapid, resulting in tremendous swelling of the seed. Optimum seed germination temperature is between 80 and 90° F. If adequate soil moisture and sunlight are present, seed germination and seedling development are swift. Mortality during this stage is generally caused by water stress due to lack of soil moisture.

Once the mesquite seedling develops its first true leaf, the mesquite stays in what is called a "juvenile stage" for two to three years, during which mature, woody tissue develops. Juvenile mesquite trees usually grow to about three feet high, depending on site conditions, species, and weather factors. In this juvenile stage, mesquite has a very thin bark and is highly susceptible to a wildfire: any fire that sweeps through the land will kill almost all of the young mesquite. Once out of this stage, with their bark and wood "hardened off," mesquite trees will survive almost any wildfire situations. Fire may kill back the wood above ground, but the root collar and lateral roots will survive, resulting in the sprouting of dormant buds located around the root collar. Mesquite trees in the juvenile stage are also very susceptible to having their terminal buds "nipped" by insects and larger animals such as skunks, raccoons, and livestock or being killed-back by severe weather such as heavy freezes. If the terminal bud is removed, multiple lateral sprouts will begin to grow from dormant buds found under the bark, resulting in a multistemmed tree. Under favorable conditions, juvenile mesquites may reach heights of six to seven feet, but mesquites in the juvenile stage usually do not flower.

Mesquite trees mature after about three years into a single-stemmed tree or a multistemmed shrub. The single-stemmed tree results from undisturbed growth in the seedling and juvenile stages. Buds near the stem's tip produce leaves; the thorns are modified stems. Dormant buds are present under the bark all along the trunk, branches, and twigs. If part of the above-ground trunk or limb is removed, these dormant buds will activate and sprouts will occur; if the whole above-ground portion of the tree is removed, numerous new stems will form from the bud zone around the ground-line rootcollar. If a mesquite tree is cut below the ground line, no sprouting will occur and it will die. Sprouts do not form from rootwood.

Once bud burst occurs in the spring, mesquite grows vigorously for six to eight weeks. Fruit development takes two to three months, although during extended wet periods throughout the summer months additional bean crops can occur. In many locations in Texas rainfall is adequate to stimulate continuous bean crops into midsummer. After midsummer, when growth has slowed, the trees are essentially dormant except for flushes of new leaves stimulated by rainy periods. In the United States mesquite trees usually begin their defoliation around the time of the first killing frost, normally sometime during November through December.

Mesquite-Water Relationships

Mesquite is a phreatophyte, a plant that has adapted itself to arid environments by growing extremely long roots to acquire water at or near the water table. Mesquite has the advantage of sending its roots deeper and farther into the soil than almost all other competing plants. The roots have been measured to extend forty-five feet downward and forty-five feet horizontally to find water. Intensive brush-covered rangeland with little grass present is reported to increase wind and soil erosion. As the site becomes drier and drier, it becomes very difficult for grass to become established and survive.

Mesquite can withstand periods of long-term drought that kill many other Southwest plants because it has an internal mechanism that allows it to reduce its water requirements as the evaporative potential of the site increases. As the weather and the site become drier, mesquite closes the stomata or pores on its leaflets and lowers its transpiration rate. This explains mesquite's ability to infest the driest of sites, where competing brush and grass species cannot obtain a foothold. Bare areas without vegetation increase as mesquite covers dry rangelands; eventually, as the brush completely engulfs a range, little grass remains.

Proponents of programs to eradicate the mesquite on Southwest rangelands in the United States justify their stance by the fact that mesquite is a "robber" of vital soil moisture that could otherwise be utilized by range grass. Indeed, mesquite is a large user of soil water; estimates are that mesquite and other brush species such as juniper, acacia, and Chinese tallow tree annually use approximately ten million acre-feet (an acre-foot is the amount of water it takes to cover an acre of land twelve inches deep) (Dahl 1982). Obviously, mesquite, which covers more than 56 million acres of Texas rangelands, is a major culprit. Mesquite's use of water may not only reduce the production of range grasses, but, in some instances, reduce the available water for agricultural irrigation and urban usage. Scientists have estimated that about 38 percent of the average annual rainfall in Texas is used by noncommercial plants, much of that by the mesquite.

Many examples exist of the water-related benefits of managing mesquite. Ranchers in the San Angelo, Texas, area noticed that natural springs that had dried up after heavy infestation of brush occurred on adjoining rangeland regained steady flow after range management began. In one instance, after having thousands of acres of rangeland cleared in the 1950s and 1960s, Dry Rocky Creek began flowing within five years after the brush clearing was completed in the 1960s after not having flowed for many years (Dahl 1982). It continues to flow today.

In another example, in the Panhandle of Texas, local authorities think that the extreme infestation of brush on rangeland over the past forty years has impeded the inflow of groundwater into Lake Meredith, the reservoir that supplies water to the cities of Lubbock and Amarillo (*Dallas Morning News*, January 1, 1997).

Mesquite's possible negative impact on the water situation of Texas rangeland must be balanced with the benefits of its presence. Mesquite adds a tremendous amount of organic matter to the soil through its leaves, pods, and woody matter and is reported to enrich the soil with nitrogen. Studies have shown that on rangelands where mesquite is one-third of the land cover, the soils contain two to three times as much organic matter as on rangelands without the presence of mesquite, and the mesquite can add thirty to one hundred pounds of nitrogen per acre per year (Felker et al. 1986). Considering that normal rainfall in Texas only adds an average of about one to four pounds of atmospheric nitrogen per acre per year, mesquite can be a vital part of the rangeland's health. Researchers have estimated that on well-managed savanna-type rangeland sites with grass and occasional mesquite trees, about 2,700 pounds of grass can be produced per acre per year, compared to about 188 pounds on an all-grass range (Felker et al. 1986). It is important to recognize the value of the mesquite to the range and to manage both the mesquite and the range grass for the betterment of the whole site.

Indeed, mesquite left unmanaged can become an unyielding pest on Texas rangelands, but in a well-designed and managed rangeland program mesquite can not only be a benefit to the productivity and health of the site but also provide added fodder and cover for livestock and wildlife during hot, dry times.

Nitrogen Fixation and Mesquite

Mesquite, like most plants of the bean family, interacts with bacterial microbes in the soil called *Rhizobium* which attach to the mesquite's roots, causing the mesquite to form nodules. The nodules appear on mesquite as swelling of the roots somewhat like root tubers. Current and past research suggests that at these nodules, in a symbiotic relationship with the mesquite, these microbes take atmospheric nitrogen from the soil and convert it to ammonia in a process called nitrogen fixation (Bailey 1976; Baird et al. 1985; Felker and Clark 1980; and Jenkins et al. 1989). This is a very ecologically significant process, as higher-level plants such as grasses and trees cannot use atmospheric nitrogen but can use ammonia (also an essential part of common commercial fertilizer). Through nitrogen fixation, the mesquite and the *Rhizobium* bacteria enrich the soil under the mesquite's canopy, thus enhancing the health and productivity of Southwest rangelands. Nitrogen fixation has been observed on mesquite trees both in the research laboratory and on the rangeland, although for many years the presence of *Rhizobium* nodules on mesquite's roots eluded researchers. Explanations for this difficulty in finding mesquite nodules were that their presence is highly dependent on soil conditions, root depths, and moisture conditions, and that they are present only during certain parts of the growing season. Given these factors, mesquite nodules have been hard to locate; basically only in the past decade have nodules been found on mesquite roots deep in the soil near the water table in a number of locations around the world—in southern California, in Mexico, in India. In mesquite's easternmost range in Texas, mesquite nodules have been found in varying sizes and in shapes ranging from round to very elongated, often branched.

The *Rhizobium* bacteria's ability to fix nitrogen on mesquite roots, producing a plant-usable form of nitrogen, is thought by ecologists to be a very important aspect benefiting the mesquite ecosystem. It has been hypothesized that clumps of mesquites act as "slow-release" tablets that fix nitrogen, accumulate it in their tissue, and slowly release it back to the soil, where it is utilized by grasses and other plants. In some mesquite ecosystems, mesquite contributes about thirty to one hundred pounds of nitrogen per acre per year (Rundel et al. 1982).

With hundreds of millions of acres of mesquite in the world, it is clear that mesquite is potentially a major contributor to the nitrogen reserve of the rangelands on which it grows. It may be that the complete eradication of mesquite would be a long-term detriment to the improvement of southwestern rangelands; this should be considered before any rangeland management brush program is initiated.

Predators of Mesquite

Mesquite is attacked by many predatory agents such as leaf, bean pod, flower, and bud insects; wood-boring beetles; domesticated livestock and wildlife; and the American mistletoe. Each affects mesquite in unique ways and in isolated instances can have a dramatic effect on the mesquite ecosystem. Given that the mesquite has greatly increased its presence on southwestern United States rangelands over the past two hundred years, predatory attacks have obviously not been a major problem. Concern does arise when predatory agents attack valuable mesquites such as ornamental landscape specimen trees or attack fine woodwork crafted from mesquite wood.

Insect Predators

Mesquite trees are attacked by many predatory insects on southwestern United States rangeland, and insects also infest mesquite wood in the rough wood form and in finished wood products. Insect attacks on mesquite trees are normal ecological occurrences that, with the germination and growth of seedlings, make the range a dynamic cyclical ecosystem. Most infestations are of such a low level that they do not have a significant effect on the mesquite ecosystem. Only in isolated cases, such as an attack on a valuable ornamental shade tree or a large buildup of a predatory insect population, is concern warranted. To prevent these instances, there is a need for continuing awareness of the risk of a predatory outbreak and then for a quick response.

Worldwide, many insects attack mesquite trees. The defoliation of both individual trees and the trees on thousands of acres of southwestern United States rangeland has occurred in the past. In spite of these isolated instances, mesquites normally respond aggressively and rebound fiercely. Insect attacks on mesquite have not yet "biologically" controlled mesquite's domination of millions of acres of rangelands in the United States and elsewhere in the world.

Mesquite predatory insects can be divided into three broad groups that feed on different parts of the tree; foliage-feeding insects; bud-, flower-, and pod-feeding insects; and insects that live in the wood and bark. Each insect has a characteristic life cycle and biology and interacts with mesquite uniquely. The degree of the effect on a tree at any particular time is dependent on the total insect populations, the presence of the insect's natural enemies, weather-related variables such as severe freezing and droughts, and the general health of the tree and of the tree population. Except in a few isolated observations, insect attacks have been kept in check by their natural predators such as insect parasites and arthropods such as spiders.

Three notable insects that feed on mesquite foliage worldwide are bagworms (*Oiketicus* spp.), cutworms (*Melipotis* spp.), and walking sticks (*Diapheromera* sp.). Only a few isolated outbreaks of defoliation by foliage feeders on significant stands of trees have ever been recorded, one instance being in 1971, when thousands of acres of mesquite in west Texas were defoliated by the cutworm, but no tree mortality resulted.

Many species of insects feed on mesquite's buds, flowers, and legume pods. Insects such as the Texas psyllid (*Heteropsylla texana*) and the western flower thrip (*Frankliniella occidentalis*) have been observed to attack with such vengeance that more than 200 psyllids have been noticed on individual terminal buds. There have not been any documented instances where bud or flower insects have caused widescale problems. Mesquite pods and seeds are consistently attacked by many insects, often causing heavy damage and making the seed nonviable for germination. Insects such as the leaf-footed bug (*Mozena obtuza*), the mesquite seed beetle (*Algarobius prosopis*, also known as the bruchid beetle), and the conchuela stick bug (*Chlorochroa ligata*) are attracted to the mesquite pod's high sugar content. Scientists have investigated cases where up to 96 percent of seeds on widespread acreage have been destroyed due to infestations by the leaf-footed bug. This insect has such an impact on mesquite seed germination in a few instances that scientists think that it could possibly be intentionally used as a biological agent to control mesquite.

Larvae of many wood-boring insects also attack mesquite, living primarily in dead and dying trees. Carpenterworm larvae can cause extensive damage to mesquite. Its larvae pupate in the wood then exit the tree, leaving the pupal skins protruding from the hole in the tree. The emerging moths are gray-mottled and black and have a wingspan of up to three inches. Adult females lay their eggs in crevices in the bark. After hatching, the borer works its way into the wood, living up to three years there and then beginning its life cycle again. During their years in the wood, the larvae continue to make large burrows running throughout the wood, often causing thc tree to be so weakened that it blows over in a windstorm.

Many other wood-infesting beetles of various insect families affect mesquite. Larvae of the roundhead borers (Cerambycidae) and the flathead borers (Buprestidae) infest both live and dead trees. Most parts of the tree can be infested and riddled with burrows, including twigs, sprouts, and seedlings; the sapwood and heartwood of large limbs; and trunks of living trees.

Other wood borers specifically attack only recently cut trees, logs, lumber, or finished wood products. One roundhead borer, the mesquite borer or longhorn beetle (*Megacyllene antennata*), is the most destructive. The reddish-brown adult is up to one inch in length and round bodied, with long legs and antennae and gray bands marked with white or gray pubescence. The adults fly early in the fall and again in the spring, placing their eggs in bark crevices of dead or dying trees and of wood that has been cut for not more than a few months. In a short time, the eggs hatch and the larvae burrow beneath the bark, enter the wood, and excavate extensive mines. Fence posts can be severely infested and damaged if cut in this "adult flying" period. Proper cutting will reduce the problem; trees cut in Texas from November 15 to January 15 will seldom be attacked.

Numerous types of wood borers carve extensive galleries in both living mesquite trees and wood after it is milled. (Photo © Ken E. Rogers)

Table 3. Common Mesquite Wood Borers: Description and Characteristics

BEETLE	APPEARANCE
Lyctid powder-post beetles (true powder-post beetle)	Adult is about ¼ inch long, slender, reddish-brown, larvae less than ¼ inch; larvae life cycle of nine to twelve months in the wood
Bostrichid powder-post beetles (false powder-post beetles)	Adult is about ½ inch long, reddish-brown to black, elongated and cylindrical; larvae life cycle of one to five years in the wood
Anobiid death watch beetles (furniture beetles)	Adult is ⅛ to ¼ inch long, reddish-brown and covered with fine yellow hairs; life cycle normally two to three years, sometimes to ten years; multiple generations in the wood; makes "ticking" sound while boring in wood
Scolytid bark beetles	Adult is ⅛ to ⅓ inch long, black or brown, cylindrical and hard-shelled; adult bores into bark, living between bark and wood, and scoring the wood surface under the bark; several generations in one year in wood
Mesquite roundhead borers (mesquite longhorn beetles)	Adult is up to 1 inch in length, round-bodied, oval in shape, and reddish-brown with gray bands marked with white or gray pubescence, and large antennae, often longer than the body; one-year life cycle
Buprestid flathead borers (mesquite branch borers)	Adult is ⅛ to ¾ inch long, with a flattened appearance, beautifully marked or metallic-colored; life cycle two to four years in wood, sometimes to twenty years
Carpenterworms	Adult is a moth, gray with black and lighter colors, with a three-inch wingspan; larvae can live three years in wood

DAMAGE	FRASS (DUST IN HOLE) AND HOLE CHARACTERISTICS
In seasoned lumber, usually in sapwood, rarely in heartwood; infests finished woodwork such as furniture, flooring, paneling	Loosely filled galleries; particles small, powdery or talclike, no pellets, small round exit holes, 1⁄32 to 1⁄16 inch in diameter; wood often crumbly
Attacks seasoned wood or finished products such as timbers, paneling, flooring, furniture; usually in sapwood	Tightly packed galleries with coarse dust, often containing wood fragments; dust sticks together, no pellets, round exit holes 3⁄32 to 9⁄32 inch in diameter
In seasoned wood and finished products; usually in sapwood, rarely in heartwood	Galleries packed with small pellets; pellets stick together, granular, small round exit holes, 1⁄16 to 1⁄8 inch in diameter; sometimes also powdery frass falling from exit holes
Usually only infests freshly killed trees; usually does not bore into wood itself and goes only a short distance into sapwood	If holes are present, galleries tightly filled with fine to coarse dust, exit holes 1⁄16 to 3⁄32 inch in diameter
Usually attacks recently felled logs and dead and dying trees, sometimes rough green lumber and living trees; usually the sapwood, rarely the heartwood	Frass is coarse to fibrous, often absent from hole; exit holes round to oval, 1⁄8 to 3⁄8 inch in diameter
Usually attacks weakened, injured, or dying trees, stumps, logs; larvae don't normally bore into the wood; usually only slightly into the sapwood and then only in lumber with bark attached	Frass is sawdustlike, tightly packed in exit hole; oval exit hole is 1⁄8 to 1⁄2 inch in diameter
Infests healthy and dying trees, often producing so many galleries that tree blows over in wind	Frass is often forced from holes in bark; dark-colored saps flow from hole

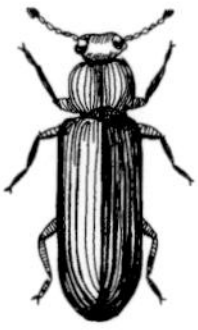

Lyctid powder-post beetles

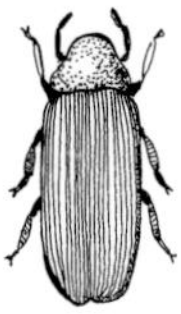

Bostrichid powder-post beetles or false powder post beetles

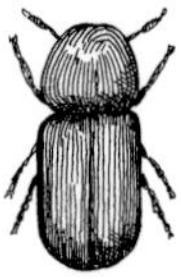

Anobiid death watch beetle

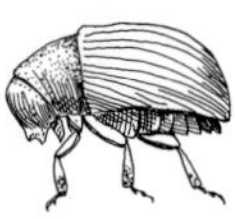

Scolytid bark beetles

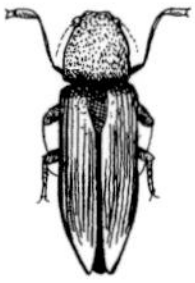

Buprestid flathead borer or mesquite branch borer

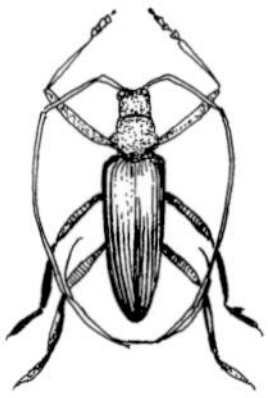

Cerambycid roundhead borer or mesquite longhorn beetle

Cossid carpenterworm

The common mesquite wood borers in dead and dying trees, green and seasoned lumber, and finished woodwork — adult images

Another roundhead borer, the mesquite girdler (*Oncideres rhodosticta*), can cause extensive damage in localized areas, in one instance girdling up to 40 percent of all limbs up to one inch in diameter.

In contrast to roundhead borers, flathead beetles have a flattened appearance and are beautifully marked or metallic-colored. Weakened, injured, or dying trees and stumps are the usual attack sites, but occasionally green trees are infested. Flathead beetle larvae usually only feed just under the bark, extending little into the sapwood. One common flathead borer, the mesquite branch borer (*Aneflus protensus*), deposits eggs in bark crevices at the forks of small living branches. The larva hollows out the stem and works its way downward through the green wood. Damage by flathead borers can be distinguished by oval tunnels, in contrast to the roundhead borers' round tunnels.

Four additional families of beetles attack mesquite wood only in the seasoned or finished state: powder-post beetles (family Lyctidae), false powder-post beetles (family Bostrichidae), death watch beetles (family Anobiidae), and bark beetles (family Scolytidae). These insects make their presence known by exit holes in the wood surface. Their larvae can reduce wood to a mass of powder or pelletized "frass" (fine wood dust) in a short period. They attack dead wood almost exclusively, especially dried, seasoned lumber and finished products. Each has distinctive life cycles and burrow-hole characteristics that aid in identification of the specific insect.

Insect infestations of mesquite trees in the natural setting are not usually significant enough to affect people or even to create any awareness of the infestation. The natural order of things is that the infestation occurs; trees are defoliated; twigs, flowers, buds, and branches are sometimes lost; and the trees replace the lost members quickly. Occasionally a tree dies; if so, replacement is quick by reseeding from adjacent trees.

Typical control of tree-feeding insects is by use of a chemical insecticide (commonly Dursban) or the natural product *Bacillus thuringiensis*. Treatment is easy and often quickly effective. Treatment for borers in the bark and wood of living trees is more difficult, but they can often be controlled with an insecticide wash of the bark and wrapping it with paper, burlap, or aluminum.

A rather original insect that affects mesquite to a limited extent is the desert termite (*Gnathamitermes tubiformans*), which occurs in southern Texas, Arizona, and New Mexico and in northern Mexico. On rangeland it attacks dead mesquite trees from March through September by forming fine dirt tubes and sheeting around the wood, not tunneling into the wood but only eating the surface material. In rare and isolated instances, fence posts and other raw wood can be affected, causing structural failure.

Killing Wood Borers in Mesquite Wood

Larvae of wood borers can inflict severe damage on a piece of woodwork, making it virtually useless. When infestation occurs, it must quickly be eradicated. Eradication is not difficult, but proper procedures must be followed to ensure killing all the larvae. The easiest way to prevent having insect problems is to reduce the risk of infestation from the outset. Infestation of seasoned lumber or unfinished woodwork can usually be prevented by quick removal of the bark after sawing; if correct guidelines are followed, most infestations can be avoided. Good sanitation procedures to keep clean, uninfected wood from rough, freshly cut logs and lumber should be followed, as adult beetles emerging from infested wood can easily fly into clean wood. When mesquite lumber drying is completed or the woodwork is crafted, it should be removed from exposure to potential infestation from rough wood. You can often prevent initial infestation by making it a habit to cut and harvest mesquite trees in the cool period of the year, in Texas from November through January, a time when the adult insects are inactive. Once cut, the wood should be used as soon as possible.

Mesquite sapwood, the yellowish wood present close to the bark of the tree, should never be used for fine woodwork because this sapwood easily becomes infested, sometimes even after the woodwork is finished. Only the heartwood should be used.

Borer presence is plainly evident when pinhole-sized holes appear in the yellow sapwood or "frass" is pushed out of the holes. If sapwood is used, it must always be kept sealed with a wood finish and wax to prevent bare wood from being exposed to potential attack.

Several things can be done to eradicate pests from a wooden object that has become infested. Placing the object in a heated environment at 130° F for five to six hours will kill all borers. Fine woodwork should

Table 4. A Schedule for Treating Mesquite Wood with Heat to Check Damage by Wood Borers

RELATIVE HUMIDITY (%)	LETHAL TEMPERATURE REQUIRED (° F)	THICKNESS OF LUMBER (IN.)	TIME TO OVERCOME LAG AFTER KILN HAS ATTAINED LETHAL TEMPERATURE (HRS.)	ADDITIONAL MARGIN OF SAFETY (HRS.)	TIME THEN HELD AT LETHAL TEMPERATURE (HRS.)	TOTAL PERIOD OF EXPOSURE AFTER KILN HAS ATTAINED REQUIRED CONDITIONS (HRS.)
100	130	1	½	½	1½	2½
		2	2	½	1½	4
		2½	3¼	½	1½	5¼
		3	4½	½	1½	6½
80	125	1	½	½	2	3
		2	2	½	2	4½
		2½	3¼	½	2	5¾
		3	4½	½	2	7
	120	1	½	1½	6	8
		2	2	1½	6	9½
		2½	3¼	1½	6	10¾
		3	4½	1½	6	12
	115	1	½	7½	30	38
		2	2	7½	30	39½
		2½	3¼	7½	30	40¾
		3	4½	7½	30	42½
60	125	1	½	1	4	5½
		2	2	1	4	7
		2½	3¼	1	4	8¼
		3	4½	1	4	9½
	120	1	½	2	7	9½
		2	2	2	7	11
		2½	3¼	2	7	12¼
		3	4½	2	7	13½
	115	1	½	9	36	45½
		2	2	9	36	47
		2½	3¼	9	36	48¼

Source: From Moore 1979.

not be exposed to this temperature, however, as it may damage the finish and split the wood. Another cure for wooden objects and for large volumes of lumber is to fumigate with magnesium or aluminum phosphide fumigants. Exposure of the wood to the fumigant in a closed container or sealed room for two days will normally kill all the larvae and adult beetles in the wood. These chemicals are poisonous, so fumigation should only be done by a licensed pest control operator following strict procedures.

Borers can be often killed by using a common household gaseous fumigant that is available at most hardware or variety stores. The gaseous fumigant is the only type that is effective—the mist type will not work. The object should be placed in a well-sealed container and exposed to the fumigant for two to three days. After treatment, the object should not be exposed to nearby untreated wood, as it can become reinfested. Another method that has proven quite successful for small woodwork is using a microwave oven. Using the defrost-cycle (about 10 percent power), heat the object for three or four five- to six-minute cycles. Be careful not to microwave objects that contain any plastic or metal decorative ornaments or fasteners and avoid overheating, as wood burns from the inside out in a microwave. Care and patience should be the watchwords.

Large Animal Predators

Almost all of the wild animals within mesquite's range use mesquite either in their normal diet or during times of drought when preferred forage plants are scarce. Quail, doves, turkeys, and ducks are a few of the birds that eat mesquite foliage, flowers, and pods. Rodents such as various rats, squirrels, and prairie dogs eat mesquite's tender sprouts, roots, and pods. Rabbits, skunks, white-tailed deer, raccoons, peccaries, and coyotes also rely on the mesquite for some of their food supply.

Many old-timers of the Southwest will tell you they know exactly why the mesquite has invaded the grassy rangelands of Texas. After watching the prairies around Haskell County in west Texas for more than fifty-three years, one man made this observation:

Many old-timers tell of years past when the prairie dogs lived across much of the Southwest, keeping the invasive mesquite under control by eating the succulent new seedlings before they got established.
(Photo © Dr. Steven Archer, Texas A&M University, College Station, Texas)

> "It's because we killed out the prairie dogs, he says." "When I came out to this country, prairie dogs had numerous towns and they scampered all over the prairies and their holes were everywhere. There were no mesquite trees, or very few. Then we had to eradicate the prairie dogs because we believed they destroyed much of our crop, so we began to poison them and then filled up their holes. Prairie dogs did not allow the tender mesquite to live, gnawing them away. And as long as prairie dogs went unmolested, there were no mesquite trees." (Lee 1986, 66)

More recently, Texas A&M University studied the effects of the prairie dog on mesquite growth (Wiltzin et al. 1997). On a fenced range in north Texas, cattle were excluded from an area containing a prairie dog colony. At various feeding stations on and off the colony three different forms of mesquite were placed: mesquite seeds and pods, planted honey mesquite seeds, and transplanted small mesquite trees.

It was found that prairie dogs removed pods and seeds and nipped and stripped bark from the young plants, causing great young seedling mortality. Researchers concluded that prairie dogs indeed may have prevented large-scale mesquite establishment on Texas rangelands (Wiltzin et al. 1997). Where the mesquite and prairie dog originally coexisted on the rangelands, the broad-scale eradication of the prairie dog could have removed a very important natural mesquite predator.

Domesticated animals and livestock such as horses, cattle, sheep, and goats also eat the mesquite's green bean pod, cherishing its high sugar content, but are much more reluctant to eat dried pods, unless they are mixed with other foods. The pods are eaten whole, with the bean usually passing through undigested, stomach acid–stratified, and readier for germination. In the past, during severe droughts, mesquite bean pods were harvested and milled into a meal and fed to livestock. Although mesquite bean pods are attractive to livestock, heavy consumption of pods sometimes has led to severe digestive disturbances, even death.

Mistletoe and Mesquite

One of the most common recognizable predators of mesquite in the southwestern United States is the American mistletoe (*Phoradendron* sp.). Mistletoe, often called injerto or Christmas mistletoe, is the very dark green growth seen in the canopy of various trees, more noticeable in the winter on deciduous hardwoods. One species, the Texas mistletoe (*Phoradendron tomentosum*), is a unisexual (each plant having only a single sex), hemiparasitic (partially parasitic) plant commonly found on hackberry (*Celtis* sp.), ash (*Fraxinus* sp.), cottonwood (*Populus* sp.), and mesquite. It grows in the United States from Oklahoma south into Mexico, from Louisiana in the east to far west Texas.

Texas mistletoe, which has small leathery-textured leaves, flowers during the winter months from late November to March, producing small white berries. Mistletoe manufactures its own food, but relies on its host the mesquite for water and minerals; it cannot live separately from the host. It primarily lives in the canopy of the mesquite and, unless it almost engulfs a tree, does not appreciably affect its growth.

Texas mistletoe infests mesquite through its 56-million-acre range in Texas. (Photo © Ken E. Rogers)

Harvesting mistletoe has become a cottage industry in Texas and Oklahoma, where it is cut, dried, packaged, and sold for traditional Christmas decorations. Mistletoe also has been used for generations in various medicines, treating ailments such as pleurisy, gout, epilepsy, rabies, and poisoning.

Traditions involving mistletoe date from ancient times, when the Druids believed that mistletoe could bestow good health and good luck on those who possess it. It has been a superstition in Western society that kissing under the mistletoe increases the possibility of marriage in the coming year. We have changed that tradition in the

United States: the hanging of mistletoe over the entryway into a room or home makes the host or hostess available to be kissed. Welsh farmers associated mistletoe with land fertility.

Texas mistletoe berries are sticky and are primarily spread by birds roosting on the mesquite's branches, who eat the berries. Birds then fly to other nearby trees, depositing seeds on new wood, where the seeds germinate. When the seed germinates, the plant develops a haustorium that penetrates into the mesquite's cambium layer just inside the bark. A haustorium is a rootlike organ produced by the mistletoe that penetrates into and absorbs nutrients from the mesquite. The mistletoe then continues to grow into a large mass of branches, relying on the tree for water and minerals. As already mentioned, except in extremely large infestations on one tree, mistletoe does not appreciably affect the health or growth of the mesquite, although in tremendously severe and rare cases it can kill a tree. If a large infestation occurs on a valuable ornamental tree, remove the mistletoe with clippers or a pruning saw, thereby eliminating the short-term risk of the tree dying. Pruning out the mistletoe plant is ineffective for long-term control, as new mistletoe growth will spring out of the point of infection. The only lasting control that has been successful for mistletoe is the physical removal of the infected limb. Pruning of infected branches should remove wood at least twelve inches below the point of entry to assure getting the whole mistletoe plant.

Many woodworkers diligently search far and wide for mesquite trees that are heavily infested with mistletoe. At the entry point of attachment the mistletoe often causes a large swelling. The wood-grain at this swelling is exceedingly variable and highly figured. This swelling, called a "mistletoe burl," contains extremely beautiful wood and is highly sought after for crafting into the most beautiful works of art.

Safety precautions should be taken when collecting and handling mistletoe berries. The berries are very poisonous and should be kept away from babies and small children. Many commercial processors of mistletoe that is targeted for home use replace the natural berries with plastic berries.

Mesquite in Texas and the Southwestern United States

Presently more than 56 million acres of mesquite ecosystem exist in Texas, 3.9 million in Oklahoma, and 22 million in Arizona and New Mexico. Limited acreage occurs in California, Colorado, Kansas, Nevada, and Utah. Of the 56 million acres in Texas, 4.3 million acres, as determined by the Soil Conservation Service's 1982 brush inventory, are classified as heavily covered, with more than 30 percent mesquite; 14.7 million acres as moderately covered, with 11 to 30 percent mesquite; and 37 million acres as lightly covered, with less than 10 percent mesquite (Soil Conservation Service 1987).

Table 5. Species of Prosopis *in the United States*

AREA	NUMBER OF SPECIES	COMMON NAME AND SPECIES
Continental United States	7	mesquite *(P. strombulifera)* creeping or dwarf mesquite *(P. reptans* var. *cinerascens)** screwbean mesquite *(P. pubescens)** mesquite *(P. articulata)* mesquite *(P. laevigata)** honey mesquite *(P. glandulosa* var. *glandulosa)** running mesquite *(P. glandulosa* var. *prostrata)** western honey mesquite *(P. glandulosa* var. *torreyana)** velvet mesquite (*P. velutina*)*
Hawaii and the Pacific Islands	2	kaiwe *(P. pallida* formae *pallida* and *armata)* mesquite *(P. juliflora)*
Puerto Rico	3	mesquite *(P. pallida)* mesquite *(P. juliflora)* mesquite *(P. glandulosa)*

Source: Developed from Burkart 1976.

*Indicates species found in Texas

In the more arid areas of the southwestern United States, seven species of mesquite exist, four of which have significantly widespread distribution: honey mesquite (*Prosopis glandulosa*), velvet mesquite (*Prosopis velutina*), screwbean mesquite (*Prosopis pubescens*), and creeping mesquite (*Prosopis reptans* var. *cinerascens*). Each species is more or less concentrated in specific areas of the Southwest, but they have widely overlapping ranges. Five of the seven species are found in Texas.

Unlike the variable appearance of the *Prosopis* species worldwide, *Prosopis* in the southwestern United States is relatively uniform, so that a general description can include all seven species. B. L. Turner, in his book *The Legumes of Texas*, gives a scientific description of the mesquites in the southwestern United States (the bracketed comments are mine).

Prosopis *(Mesquite)*

> Low, woody shrubs or small trees, usually armed with straight stout spines [thorns]. Leaves with one to several pairs of pinnae [petiole-like division of the leaf] and mostly numerous, narrow leaflets. Flowers in globose [ball-like] heads or cylindric spikes [flowers located on one elongated axis or stem], yellowish or yellowish-brown; anthers bearing apical glands [the polleniferous portion of the stamen bearing small appendages]. Fruit is a straight or tightly coiled indehiscent [does not open when ripe] pod. Basic chromosome number, as determined from counts on 11 species, x=14 (D. & W.) [C. D. Darlington and A. P. Wylie, *Chromosome Atlas of Flowering Plants* (New York: Macmillan, 1956)]. (Turner 1959, 34)

Of the mesquites in the United States, honey mesquite (*Prosopis glandulosa*) occurs in all of the nine states listed above but is primarily found in Texas, Arizona, and New Mexico. In Texas honey mesquite is found in all regions except the extreme eastern Pineywoods. The specific epithet *glandulosa* refers to the glandular anther connections of the flowers. Three varieties of honey mesquite have been identified, one being the typical variety *Prosopis glandulosa* var. *glandulosa.* The leaves on honey mesquite are long-petiole, compounded of two (occasionally three or four) pairs of pinnae with twelve to twenty leaflets on each. Its leaflets are smooth and narrow in shape, about ¾ to 2½ inches in length and about ½-inch wide. Its pods are straight, yellowish-brown, and 4 to 9 inches long. Honey mesquite's flowers are spikes 2 to 7 inches in length. Besides its typical form, var. *glandulosa*, two other varieties of honey mesquite are recognized: western honey mesquite and running mesquite. Western honey mesquite (*Prosopis glandulosa* var. *torreyana*) differs from variety *glandulosa* in that it has shorter leaflets, ½ to 1 inch in length, which are much closer to each other. Its general geographical range is limited to the Trans-Pecos and the south Texas high plains region of western Texas, westward to California. Running mesquite (*Prosopis glandulosa* var. *prostrata*) is a smaller form of honey mesquite that differs from both honey mesquite and western honey mesquite in that it has strong underground horizontal branches, with its above-ground branches being very prostrate, never or seldom arborescent (treelike). Running mesquite primarily grows in the same regions of Texas and the southwestern United States as the typical variety of honey mesquite.

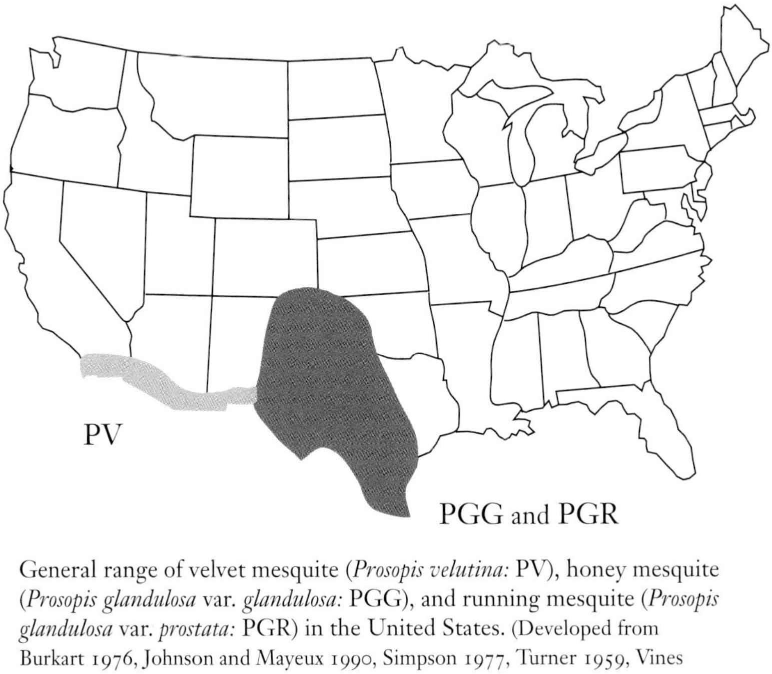

General range of velvet mesquite (*Prosopis velutina:* PV), honey mesquite (*Prosopis glandulosa* var. *glandulosa:* PGG), and running mesquite (*Prosopis glandulosa* var. *prostata:* PGR) in the United States. (Developed from Burkart 1976, Johnson and Mayeux 1990, Simpson 1977, Turner 1959, Vines 1976, and other sources)

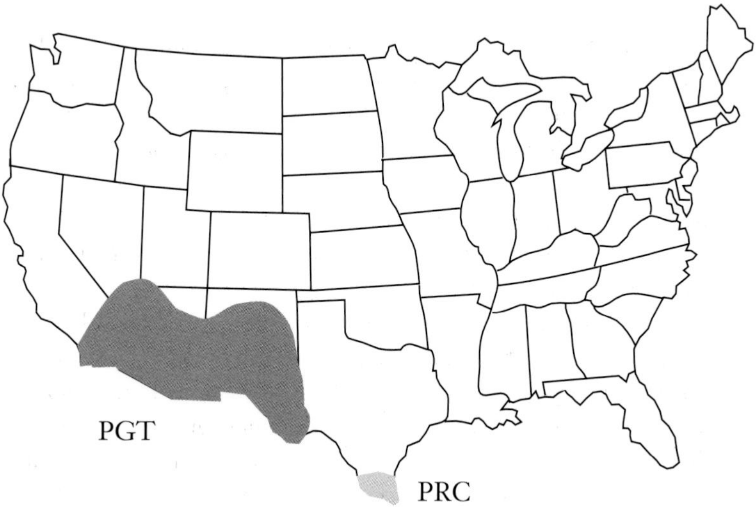

General range of western honey mesquite (*Prosopis glandulosa* var. *torreyana:* PGT), and creeping or dwarf mesquite (*Prosopis reptans* var. *cinerascens:* PRC) in the United States. (Developed from Burkart 1976, Johnson and Mayeux 1990, Simpson 1977, Turner 1959, Vines 1976, and other sources)

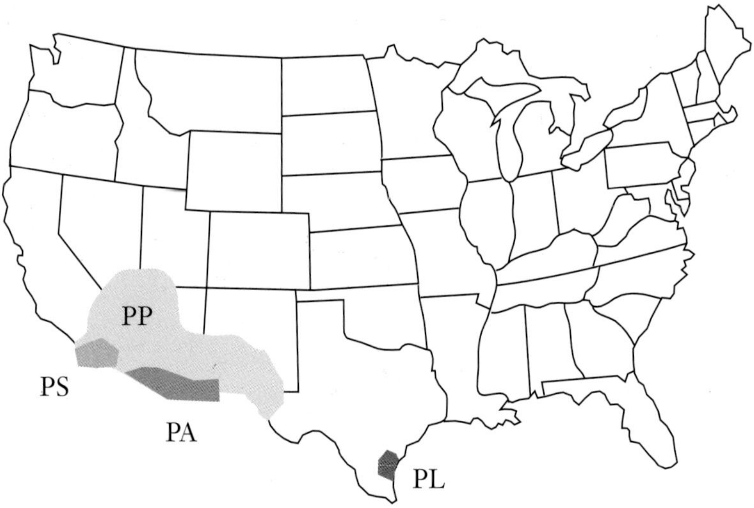

General range of screwbean mesquite (*Prosopis pubescens:* PP), *Prosopis laevigata* (PL), *Prosopis strombulifera* (PS), and *Prosopis articulata* (PA) in the United States. (Developed from Burkart 1976, Johnson and Mayeux 1990, Simpson 1977, Turner 1959, Vines 1976, and other sources)

Another species, velvet mesquite (*Prosopis velutina*), gets its common and species names from its finely haired leaves and pods. Normally in three or four pairs of pinnae, its leaflets are smaller than those of honey mesquite, being ⅕ to ½ inch in length, twelve to thirty per pinna. Velvet mesquite's pods, similar in length to honey mesquite's, are flattened, straight, and very velutinous. Its flowers are ⅕- to ½-inch long spikes. Velvet mesquite's range is confined to southern Arizona, southern New Mexico, far southwest Texas, and the adjacent portion of California and northern Mexico. A third species, screwbean mesquite (*Prosopis pubescens*), obtained its common name from its tightly coiled pods. The specific epithet *pubescens* refers to its hairy fruit. Its range is limited to the Trans-Pecos region of Texas westward through southern California and northward to Utah and Nevada. Screwbean mesquite's leaves usually have one pair of pinnae, and its leaflets are in four to eight pairs per pinna, pubescent, and ⅙ to ½ inch long and ⅒ to ⅕ inch broad. Its flowers are 2- to 3-inch spikes. A fourth species, creeping or dwarf screwbean mesquite (*P. reptans* var. *cinerascens*), has a growth form that is much different from the others: it is a very low lying, "creeping" shrub. Dwarf screwbean's specific epithet, *reptans*, literally means "creeping." Its leaves have one pair of pinnae, and its leaflets, about 1 inch in length, are close together, often touching, six to twelve pairs per pinna. Its yellow pods are tightly coiled in nine to twelve coils, similar to screwbean mesquite's pods. In contrast to screwbean's spike flower, creeping mesquite's flower is a reddish globe. Dwarf screwbean mesquite's range is limited to the southwest Rio Grande plains of Texas and adjacent locations in northern Mexico.

Three other less-known and less widely distributed species of mesquite grow in the continental United States. One, *Prosopis strombulifera*, grows only in Imperial County, California, where it was brought from Peru and escaped cultivation. Its pod is a tight coil, and its leaves have one pair of pinnae with leaflets in three to eight pairs per pinna, ¾ to 1¼ inch long. Its flower is a yellow globe or ball, ½ inch in diameter. Another mesquite, *Prosopis laevigata*, has a range in the United States limited to a few trees in Nueces County, Texas. Its pod is dry and flattened, 4 to 10 inches in length. It has one or two pairs of pinnae, each having twenty to thirty pairs of linear to elliptically shaped leaflets, ⅒ to ½ inch long. The flowers are yellow, 2- to 4-inch spikes. A seventh mesquite species, *Prosopis articulata*, is located in the United States in a limited area of southernmost Arizona. Its pods are dry, compressed, and extremely constricted between the seeds. Its leaves have one to two pairs of pinnae with five to twenty pairs of leaflets each, and its flowers are 2- to 5-inch spikes.

Identification Key to the Prosopis *Species in the Southwestern United States*

(Adapted from Burkart 1976 and Simpson 1977)

1 Spines beige or brown, arising above a leaf cluster, or solitary and axillary or formed by branch tips. Inflorescence a spike or a slender catkin. Flowers white to dull yellow or red. Pods straight or loosely spireled, usually somewhat fattened. Seeds in pods arranged end to end and separated by a tough, stony endocarp. 2

1 Spines white or yellow, arising from underneath a leaf cluster and formed by stipules that have become spiny. Inflorescence in round heads or in open stubby spikes. Pods coiled in several planes or short, stubby arched, leaves always only one pair of pinnae and small leaflets. 7

  2 Pods straight, without visible beading. 3

  2 Pods slightly beaded, usually speckled. 4

3 Aerial branching arborescent, nor prostrate. No underground horizontal branching. Texas through California, Oklahoma, southeastern Colorado, southeastern Utah, New Mexico, Arizona, southern Nevada. Running mesquite, *Prosopis glandulosa* var. *prostrata*

  4 Leaves expanded, lax, usually longer than inflorescence. 5

  4 Leaves small, shorter than or equal to inflorescence. Extreme southern Arizona. Mesquite, *Prosopis articulata*

5 Leaflets ⅛ to 2½ inches, linear or oblong in outline, never ovate. 6

Beginning around the start of the twentieth century, mesquite greatly increased its presence on southwestern United States rangelands. It went from a vital resource to a strong adversary competing for limited water resources. Before this time mesquite, although present on the southwestern ranges, had limited coverage, mainly growing in the moist

5 Leaflets elliptic oblong in outline, glabrous and less than 7/16 inch long, 12 to 30 per pinna. Pod straight and beaded or with parallel edges. Southern Texas in Nueces County. Mesquite, *Prosopis laevigata*

6 Leaflets pubescent, or if glabrous over 7/16 inch long and separated from one another, 3/16 to 5/8 inch long and 1/16 to 3/16 inch wide, 1 to 4 pairs per pinna. Arizona and adjacent California. Velvet mesquite, *Prosopis velutina*

6 Leaflets glabrous, or only slightly ciliate along the margins, large 7/16 to 2½ inches long, widely separated along the rachis, the distance between them equal to, or greater than, the width of the leaflet. Eastern Arizona, New Mexico, and western Texas. Western honey mesquite, *Prosopis glandulosa* var. *torreyana*

7 Inflorescence an open spike of yellow flowers, pods with numerous coils. Texas Big Bend country to California, north to Utah/Nevada. Screwbean mesquite, *Prosopis pubescens*

7 Inflorescence globose or ovoid in shape, less than 7/16 inch in diameter. 8

8 Leaflets widely spaced along the rachis, 3 to 8 pairs per pinna, glabrous. Only in Imperial County, California. Mesquite, *Prosopis strombulifera*

8 Leaflets close together, almost overlapping, usually 6 to 12 pairs per pinna, glabrous or variously pubescent. Trans-Pecos Region of Texas. Creeping or dwarf mesquite, *Prosopis reptans* var. *cinerascens*

creeks and draws. Many writers of early times in the Southwest give credence to mesquite's invasion. When Colonel Randolph B. Marcy made his explorations in the Red River country in 1852, becoming the first westward explorer to see Palo Duro Canyon in the Texas Panhandle, he passed through one village of prairie dogs that he estimated covered 400,000 acres and commented that the "mesquite flats, with trees standing at wide intervals upon ground covered with a dense carpet of verdure, made a strong impression upon my eyes." Marching in 1846 with Zachary Taylor's army to invade Mexico during the Mexican War, Lieutenant Ulysses S. Grant saw the miles and miles of country between Corpus Christi and the Rio Grande as "rolling prairie, vision limited only by the earth's curvature" (Dobie 1943, 209). Today most of the prairies that Taylor's army traversed are covered with mesquite: the only vision is of the top of mesquite brush. Author Viktor Bracht in his classic *Texas in 1848* penned a revealing description of the south Texas rangelands: "As it is known, the East has more extensive forests than the West, where at most only one-third of the area is forested; sometimes only one-fourth. The rest is open prairie with scattered groves. Besides the forests along the banks of the streams, one finds extensive areas of post oak, others of mesquite of varying extent . . ." (Bracht 1931, 41).

Researchers have concluded that mesquite has essentially the same growing range today as it had in the early 1800s, spreading perhaps slightly northward into parts of north Texas, Oklahoma, and Kansas. During the second half of the nineteenth century, after intensive cattle husbandry began, mesquite greatly increased its presence on southwestern rangelands from a few scattered groves of trees to spreading all across the rangeland. Mesquite choked out less-competitive native grasses and shrubs. Through the early years of the twentieth century mesquite rapidly invaded all open spaces and quickly became a scourge to ranch owners. It is humorous to read how the "thoughts of the day" changed during these times. In Arizona in 1906 scientists stated that they saw no indication of problems from the increase in the spread of mesquite; but by 1936 ranchers were begging the United States government for aid to help eradicate the godforsaken pest. This "mesquite jungle," as they called it, was so extensive that during roundups cattle had to be hunted for days—the mesquite thorns were agony for the cowboys and their horses.

Ranchers, unbeknownst to themselves, largely provided the vehicle for mesquite's spread from the lowland creeks to all of the grassland within its current range. During the massive cattle drives to feed Easterners' insatiable hunger for western beef, livestock would eat and digest the sweet mesquite pods. Subsequent dropping of the indigestible seeds along the cattle trails assisted in increasing mesquite's spread northward and its intensity on many grasslands where it had been found only in the lower, moister sites.

The mesquite infestation has become so bad that the United States Department of Agriculture (USDA) has officially labeled five mesquite species as dangerous "noxious weeds," and their dissemination in the United States may reasonably be expected to have a serious effect on ecosystems. A permit is required for any movement of these species into or through the United States.

In this battle, called the "Great Mesquite Wars," mesquite has continued to concentrate on Southwest rangelands, fought by the ranchers with little success. Past efforts and current research have targeted mechanical methods and equipment to cut, shave, shear, rip out, and pull out the mesquite. Chemical formulations of herbicides and growth hormones have been developed that have had some success in at least controlling mesquite's spread. Spot-treatments, boom-sprayers treating multiple trees at a time, and aerial spraying approaches have all been used to thwart the "mighty mesquite." Research at Texas A&M University, at Texas Tech University, and at Texas A&M University at Kingsville (previously Texas A&I University) began in the early 1900s, first to try to understand mesquite's growth and competitiveness and then to develop systems and procedures for its control and management. The Texas Agricultural Experiment Station's Brush Research effort at Temple has for years worked on the problem of mesquite, juniper, and prickly pear control. Current research at this station is investigating the potential and options of biological control agents such as leaf-feeding insects to control mesquite "naturally." Benefits and drawbacks of this approach have to be weighed and seriously considered before initiating large-scale biological control programs.

Researchers at the Texas Forest Service's Forest Products Laboratory have been investigating mesquite utilization since the mid-1940s, approaching this adversary as a resource. Through their efforts the use of mesquite wood for furniture, flooring, sculptures, wood turn-

Many wood sculptors of the Southwest incorporate three of the notable icons of the old days into their art: the omnipresent mesquite, the American Indian, and the American bald eagle. (Photo © Charlie Boren, master wood sculptor, Burleson, Texas)

ings, and other fine wood products has developed a loyal following in the Southwest, especially in Texas. Two or three hundred entrepreneurs have developed product lines and techniques in crafting fine woodwork from mesquite, giving it much national acclaim. Mesquite has attracted great interest from architectural and interior design associations as well as woodworking and trade organizations such as the National Hardwood Lumber Association, National Wood Flooring Association, the American Association of Furniture Artists, and the American Association of Woodturners.

Mesquite is becoming the United States' "exotic wood": many designs use mesquite as a replacement for rainforest hardwoods that have become scarce, are prohibited from being imported into the United States, or have just fallen politically out of favor with many users. Mesquite fits into a "niche" market to replace woods such as rosewood, teak, and purpleheart, from both an aesthetic and a performance standpoint (where mesquite is exceptional). Mesquite is an exquisite wood.

In the Southwest mesquite has become the wood of choice for outdoor barbecuing. In 1996 mesquite chips, chunks, mini-logs, and sawdust were reported to be more than a twenty-million-dollar industry. Seven or eight small cooking-wood processors ship mesquite barbecue wood products all over the United States and the world.

Mesquite is slowly changing from being a pest range plant to being a forest resource and the raw material for more than 250 entrepreneurs in the Southwest. Stimulated by this business activity, two associations have developed over the past fifteen years, enabling industry members to associate with each other. Los Amigos del Mesquite (the friends of the mesquite) is an international organization that supplies vital marketing programs and wood-processing information to its members. Los Amigos has aided in developing grading standards for mesquite lumber and wood flooring, has taken the lead in developing large-scale initiatives in marketing and product development, and has assisted in formulating rangeland management guidelines.

The Texas Mesquite Association is a group of more than 300 fine wood craftspersons creating works of art such as flooring, furniture, sculptures, wood turnings, and bandsawn boxes. These entrepreneurs and hobbyists use the association as a multifaceted vehicle for sharing the "mesquite mystique" and their love of the wood, as a forum for ideas and woodworking techniques, and as a marketing channel for their wares. The Texas Mesquite Association's annual wood art festival takes place at Fredericksburg, Texas, every October, attracting more than 100 mesquite artisans who set up booths to sell and "show off" their unique mesquite items to tens of thousands of visitors. Items for sale range from a $1 mesquite Christmas tree ornament to a $6,000 wood sculpture or rocking chair.

Mesquite in Hawaii

Mesquite was introduced into Hawaii in early 1828 when a Catholic priest, Father Bachelot, planted a tree at the corner of his church in downtown Honolulu which he had raised from a seed he brought with him from the Jardin du Roi in Paris. Subsequent cultivation, growth, and spread of mesquite was so prolific that by 1840 mesquite became the principal shade tree of Honolulu.

Today there are more than 150,000 acres of mesquite forest in the Hawaiian Islands, and most trees are descendant from this one tree, identified as *Prosopis pallida.* A number of other mesquite species have been imported into Hawaii by the USDA; they have been widely planted and have escaped cultivation. In Hawaii mesquite is considered the most valuable introduced tree. Its flowers are highly prized as the most important source of pure honey, and the pods are of great value as food for all kinds of livestock.

Mesquite, called kiawe in Hawaii, grows most aggresively in the leeward coastal areas, which have annual rainfall of ten to thirty inches. Kiawe rarely extends above an elevation of 5,000 feet due to the increased rainfall and the reduced temperatures, giving other plant species decided advantages. Kiawe is killed at temperatures of 21° F, much higher than the average killing temperature of mesquite species growing in the southwestern United States. On the islands of Lanai, Kahoolawe, and Niihau, it occupies vast areas on both the leeward and windward shores, forming forest belts from sea level to an altitude of 800 to 1,000 feet.

Kiawe flowers in Hawaii when three to four years old at any time of the year, but most commonly from January to March.

During wet periods it will flower a second time, usually in September and October. flowers are pale-yellow spikes three to four inches long. Kiawe pods ripen about six months after flowering, falling to the ground in April through July, where a black beetle *(Mimosestes amicus)* destroys much of the seed. The pods are usually broader, flatter, and less constricted than those found in the southwestern United States. When ground into a cattle meal, the pods produce such a weight gain in cattle that Kiawe is considered by some in Hawaii one of the "King Crops of the World."

Unlike mesquite in the southwestern United States, Kiawe in Hawaii is considered to be a shallow-rooted tree and is subject to wind-throw. This wind damage is usually limited to shallow-rooted mesquite growing in high-rainfall areas. When grown in dry areas, kiawe is well rooted like its continental cousins.

The principal use of kiawe in Hawaii is a cover crop for erosion control on arid land. It is also used extensively as a honey tree, with large volume of Hawaiian kiawe honey being exported overseas. Kiawe's durable heartwood, due to its fine hardness and stability, is the traditional wood in Hawaii for boat-builder's caulking mallets and is preferred for cement floats. Kiawe is worked into fine furniture and wood turnings by many craftspersons in Hawaii. The original kiawe tree planted by Father Bachelot in 1828, died in October 1919 at the age of 91 (Judd 1920).

Many ongoing programs seek to develop management techniques and plans for mesquite on Southwest rangeland. Mesquite has become such a valuable and beautiful resource that mesquite "forest plantations" are being considered in several locations in Texas, especially along the Gulf Coastal Bend. In many areas large mesquites of sawmill size (those from which logs more than twelve inches in diameter can be cut) are becoming scarce. The interest in mesquite for products such as flooring, furniture, and barbecue wood has created a demand for it. Although mesquite must be managed in it ecosystem, when controlled it can become a vital resource. In the not-too-distant future we will see planted and managed mesquite forests just as we see hardwood and pine forests in east Texas and in other places in the United States.

Dr. Peter Felker, a notable *Prosopis* researcher, offers the following solution, with which I concur:

> Prune and culture large mesquites on a thirty- to fifty-foot spacing so grass can grow beneath the trees with the added benefit of mesquite's soil enriching properties. Then harvest the carefully cared for trees cut on a 30 to 40 year rotation for veneer logs and luxury quality timber. . . . (Felker, personal communication, May 1987)

Mesquite will have its day in the sun.

Management of Mesquite on Southwestern United States Rangelands

As mentioned previously, on southwestern rangelands the mesquite is just one element of a very complex ecosystem that also includes other woody plants such as the legume acacia (*Acacia* spp.); livestock and large wildlife species such as the white-tailed deer; cacti such as prickly pears; microbes in the soil; various smaller animals such as birds, mammals, reptiles, and insects; and the soil itself, with all its unique physical characteristics and components. Each of these elements makes significant contributions to the health and vitality of the mesquite ecosystem. Management of the mesquite ecosystem that alters one aspect can cause widescale and significant positive or negative changes in other aspects.

Many researchers over the past decade or so have concluded that the optimal healthy mesquite ecosystem consists of a savanna-type arrangement of "mother" mesquite trees spaced thirty to fifty feet apart on grass rangeland. This type of ecosystem allows a lot of grass to grow with the mesquite, which contributes organic matter through leaf and pod fall, nitrogen (through the symbiotic relationship with nitrogen-fixing *Rhizobium* bacteria), and cooling shade and cover for livestock and wildlife. This is very important since semiarid and arid southwestern United States ranges are usually very low in organic matter and nitrogen, both essential for a healthy range. The soil under the "mother" mesquite is an island of fertility. It is interesting to note that early travelers venturing across mesquite rangelands in south Texas saw a landscape with large, scattered mesquite trees interspersed with a few smaller woody plants and extensive stretches of tall prairie grass.

In past years intense, widespread, and frequent wildfires reduced the brush intensification of the mesquite ecosystem. Fires killed all smaller, thin-barked woody plants that were invading the grasslands, whereas larger trees with thick bark were not killed.

Today, if left unattended, a savanna-type mesquite ecosystem will eventually change into a thick, almost impassable, mesquite brush forest. Under the "mother" mesquite trees in the highly fertile, nitrogen-rich, cool soil, mesquite seeds will germinate and, along with other plant species such as acacia and prickly pears, will begin to fill the space under the mesquite canopy. These smaller trees will grow, eventually forming a clump of mesquite brush. These clumps will continue to expand until adjacent clumps merge, forming a severely brush-infested site that is very unproductive for almost all livestock, wildlife, and recreational use. Many rangelands in Texas and in the southwestern United States are at this stage in their evolution. Proper management through prescribed burning, selective brush removal, and livestock stocking balance can reduce the probability of the mesquite ecosystem ever getting to this extremely brush-infested state.

One "best" management scheme for all mesquite rangeland does not exist. The objectives and goals have to be considered when developing a management plan for a particular site. If optimal livestock production is the goal, then a savanna-type system with a few large mesquite trees may be desired. On the other hand, if optimal wildlife management for recreational hunting and wildlife viewing is the goal, then strips or clumps of thick brush cover placed throughout the grass rangeland may be better. If maximum timber production is the goal, then a savanna-type range with large trees closer together than in a savanna managed for livestock production may maximize timber volumes and be the most desirable. A management plan for a particular site should also consider the capability of the site. Extremely dry, rocky sites may not be the most suitable areas for managing optimal grass for livestock production, but may be very suitable for wildlife hunting and viewing. In contrast, a moist, more fertile bottomland range may be optimal for both grass and timber production.

Today various methods are used for the control and management of mesquite on rangelands. Control methods can be divided into four general groups: prescribed burning, mechanical control, chemical control, and biological control by selective grazing. Also, biological control with predatory insects and disease-causing organisms is being researched extensively, but has not yet been accepted as a treatment technique. The most effective management approach, called Integrated Brush Management, often combines several of these methods to meet the objectives of maintaining a healthy, productive mesquite ecosystem.

Prescribed Burning

The shift from the savanna-type rangelands observed by early travelers in the 1700s and 1800s in Texas and the southwestern United States to the dense, impassable brush that is often found today was partly caused by the reduction or elimination of wild prairie fires that once were widespread and frequent. These intense fires roared through thousands and thousands of acres of rangeland, preventing mesquite seedlings and juvenile trees and other woody species from growing to a number and size that would create dense brush.

Over the past hundred years, negative experiences with wildfires have led to an incorrect assumption by the general population that suppressing all range fires is wise range management. Indeed, many wildfires have caused widespread death of range trees and grass and damage to structures. However, these were uncontrolled wildfires. As often happens, an overreaction to a potentially positive tool has almost eliminated the use of prescribed burning as a management tool. Many, many benefits of properly managed prescribed burning exist. Burning a range every two to three years increases the range forage quality, helps in bringing back desirable plant species that have disappeared with the densification of brush species, kills many animal parasites, and greatly increases the quality of plant species available for livestock and wildlife. Prescribed burning also greatly extends the effective beneficial duration of mechanical and chemical brush-control methods.

Prescribed burning can be one of the most effective tools for the range manager. Rangeland management researchers C. J. Scifres and

W. T. Hamilton in their book *Prescribed Burning for Brushland Management* offer a great summary statement supporting the use of prescribed burning: "Therefore, a major role for prescribed burning is to lend a competitive edge to herbaceous plants rather than to rid the landscape of brush . . . Properly applied, prescribed burning is a potent management tool for maintaining the herbaceous phase in shrublands following control by mechanical, chemical, or biological methods" (Scifres and Hamilton 1993, 123).

Mechanical Control

Several equipment configurations are available for effective mechanical control. Mesquite can be controlled mechanically either as lone scattered plants or by treatment of dense stands. The costs of mechanical methods are great in comparison to other methods, but control lasts longer.

Hand grubbing out individual plants is one of the oldest methods known and is still the preferred method when only a few isolated mesquites need removal. With cases of moderate or dense stands, hand grubbing becomes too laborious and expensive. In the 1930s equipment to mechanically remove mesquite was investigated by the King Ranch; in 1949, after fifteen years of experimentation with several prototypes, the root plow was developed. A root plow or root cutter is mounted on a large crawler tractor that powers the ten- to sixteen-foot V-shaped blade, severing the roots of nearly all mesquites and other brush species. If followed by reseeding, on most sites root plowing will kill some 80 to 90 percent of the mesquites. Disking and reseeding should be done as soon as possible after the land clearing is completed.

Power grubbing with large dozers was the preferred method of mechanical removal for years. The mesquites were removed below the lowest dormant bud with a large crawler tractor equipped with a front-mounted, U-shaped "stinger" blade. The time required to grub mesquite with this method was about one-half acre per hour, depending on site conditions, size of the trees, density of the stand, and weather conditions. It is most effective when soils are moist and the trees can be removed deep enough to prevent regrowth. Retreatment is usually necessary to remove small plants and regrowth sprouts that were missed.

Another common method is brush removal by "chaining," using a 200- to 300-foot chain dragged between two crawler tractors. This chain, weighing 15,000 to 20,000 pounds, uproots most of the large trees in its path, leaving the smaller, multistemmed mesquite. Chaining offers only temporary control, as many trees are broken at the ground line and profuse regrowth sprouting occurs.

Two negatives of mechanical methods of mesquite control are that they require large capital outlays in equipment and often generate strong negative responses from persons observing the cleared site.

Chemical Control

Control of mesquite with various chemicals has been attempted with varying degrees of success. In the early 1920s sodium arsenite was used as a herbicide, but its use was halted after its severe toxicity to both humans and livestock was determined. Kerosene and diesel fuel applications were two other early chemical controls: after a cut was made at the base of a mesquite, a pint or so was applied to the cut, resulting in the death of the tree. Regrowth occurred regularly, however, and retreatment was necessary every three to five years.

In the 1950s discovery of growth-regulating herbicides such as 2,4,5-T expanded the chemical control applications on mesquite. This herbicide was mixed with oil and sprayed on the bark or foliage of the mesquite, killing the tree. Eventually aerial application methods for 2,4,5-T were developed and became the most effective means. Many other effective herbicides such as Picloram and Dicamba were formulated. Today several other growth regulator herbicides are also available, with varying degrees of effectiveness. Many of these new herbicides are safer for humans and the environment than those of the past.

Spray treatments can be applied to an individual tree's foliage and are quite successful. Such treatments are usually most effective in the late spring or early summer. Soil treatments can be used, with the herbicides in the form of pellets. This is quite effective with some herbicides, but their cost is extremely high. Both ground spraying equipment and aerial application can be used for broadcasting herbicides. Since the effectiveness of a herbicide depends on its absorption and subsequent translocation throughout the tree, many factors determine whether a particular treatment is successful. Most effective herbicide treatments are made in the late spring, about two to three months after bud opening, as the maximum translocation takes place at this time and the trees have a minimum percentage of food reserve sugars.

For effective and economical control, combinations of mechanical and herbicide methods probably will be more satisfactory than any single treatment. No single method will give effective economical control under all conditions. Many factors affect the effectiveness of a mechanical or chemical treatment: density of infestation, rainfall, soils, topography, condition of brush, and the potential productivity of rangelands must all be considered.

Whatever the intensity and the effectiveness of the control methods used, reinfestation of mesquite will occur. Failure to control limited mesquite reinfestations reduces the benefits of the initial control treatment and may sometimes aggravate the brush problem. Local or regional specialists should be contacted to identify the correct control treatment for specific rangeland situations. Herbicides must be used carefully, following the handling and mixing instructions exactly.

A word of caution is necessary here. The increased use of herbicides in agricultural and forestry has caused concerns about the damage these compounds can do to humans and to the environment. Damage to the environment can occur through herbicide mist drift during application, runoff from treated areas, careless flushing of equipment during cleanup, and misapplication of herbicides across land boundaries. Extreme care should always be taken to evaluate whether a herbicide is necessary for brush control in a particular application. Proper mixing, application, disposal of unused chemicals and containers, storage, and transportation are critical to minimize the effect. When used properly, herbicides can be effective tools to control pest brush species.

Selective Grazing

Much brush infestation and reinfestation after clearing, including mesquite, can be greatly controlled by grazing domestic livestock such as goats, sheep, and cattle as a biological control agent. Young, tender seedlings and sprouts of many woody browse species like mesquite and acacia are the preferred browse of goats. Goats released on a recently cleared range that contains large mesquite will keep the seedling and sprout growth to a minimum. Goats are much more effective than sheep, which prefer forbs, and cattle, which prefer grass to woody plants.

One ranch near Henrietta, Texas, has found a novel method of brush control. You may think that you have been transported to the Middle East. Interspersed among the cattle is a herd of camels. The camels devour most of the mesquite brush, eating all the leaves, stems, and bud sprouts and thus preventing the mesquite from regenerating from seedlings or from sprouts. Although probably not a long-term solution to the brush problem on millions of acres of Texas rangelands, this is a workable, novel approach.

Biological Control with Predatory Insects and Disease-Causing Organisms

There is great potential for establishing control of mesquite on rangelands by use of a biological agent such as an insect or a fungus. Biological control means that a foreign or domestic insect or fungus is intentionally introduced into a rangeland situation in sufficiently large numbers to control the growth and spread of mesquite brush. The objective may not be to eradicate all the mesquite on the range, but to control it, reducing its economic impact.

More than three hundred species of insects have been identified that infest mesquite in North and South America, targeting many parts such as the seed, flower, bud, foliage, or limbs and trunk. Research into various insects' biological control potential has shown that the two most promising insects are the leaf-footed bug (*Mozena obtuza*) and the cutworm (*Melipotis imdomita*). These two insects, and others that may command consideration, attack the foliage of mesquite trees in the southwestern United States, Hawaii, and Puerto Rico. Various seed-feeding beetles in the Bruchidae family which attack mesquite seeds with great success are also considered potential biological control agents for mesquite. One example of an attempt to control mesquite biologically is in Australia, where a recently initiated program to assist in combating the encroaching mesquite on rangeland uses two mesquite seed–feeding bruchid beetles, *Algarobius prosopis* and *Algarobius battimeri.*

Although using biological control insects to "manage" mesquite on rangelands may be possible, care must be taken not to introduce an insect or fungus that will significantly attack beneficial plants. Two instances of extremely damaging accidental introductions of biological agents are well known from the past: the American chestnut fungus that essentially wiped out the American chestnut trees nationwide and the introduction of a beetle and a fungus that it carries, which eliminated much of the American elm population in the United States. A fine line exists between beneficial and harmful when it comes to changing the natural way of things.

Mesquite's Role in Wildlife Management

In contrast to the negative impact of dense mesquite brush on rangeland grass production, thick range brush is often a vital component of the habitat of most wildlife animals in the southwestern United States. Due to its great density potential and widespread range, mesquite is one of the most important wildlife brush species. Many wild animals such as deer, javelina, feral hogs, coyotes, wild turkeys, and quail use mesquite basically for three purposes: food, cover, and moisture. As a food source mesquite supplies subsistence from its leaves as a browse and its pods as a source of protein. Mesquite beans are not only high in protein and energy but, maybe more importantly, are very predictable annual crops. Unlike many other range plants, mesquite often puts on its greatest pod crop in the driest years, becoming a "last resort" or emergency food during the worst of droughts for wildlife struggling for survival.

Mesquite provides a high-quality browse and a much more dependable food supply during dry periods when compared with weeds and grasses. Mesquite leaves are 16 to 19 percent crude protein, far greater than the maintenance level of 6 to 7 percent for white-tailed deer (Beasom 1988). The availability of large volumes of quality browse makes Texas a premier habitat for many wildlife species such as the white-tailed deer.

Mesquite also provides wildlife cover, functioning as a "thermal shade" in the stifling hot summer months. Large, widely spaced mesquites with their long, spreading branches provide excellent shade for deer. Smaller mesquites provide essential understory cover for smaller animals such as quail and turkeys. Perennial grass stands decline with the invasion and increased density of mesquite, but the removal of all trees is very detrimental to some wildlife species. Leaving a percentage of thick brush mesquite in strips or preferably in patches increases wildlife forage and improves their habitat.

For both wildlife hunting and wildlife viewing management, the optimum intensity of mesquite varies with individual wildlife species. Deer, quail, mourning doves, and other game and nongame animals prefer a certain level of brush cover and have dramatically different needs. Many wildlife species, such as the white-tailed deer, prefer varying degrees of brush cover for browsing, escape and security, travel, and birthing or nesting. Placing different densities of brush on a range may be the best wildlife management scheme. Recent studies have shown that the maximum population of white-tailed deer can be retained on rangeland with an average of 60 percent brush cover, whereas quail populations do best with only about 5 to 10 percent brush cover. Compounding the issue, the amount of brush cover preferred by each wildlife species depends greatly on soil type, topography, and plant species present (Beasom 1988). Intensive range management practices such as root plowing and chaining decrease the value of rangelands for white-tailed deer by reducing the density of the brush and the number of browse species. In one instance in Bastrop, Texas, the elimination of heavy brush along the creek bottoms caused several herds of deer to leave the site, looking for more adequate cover.

Managing rangelands as a wildlife habitat can be quite satisfying and very profitable for Southwest ranchers. Many ranchers are looking at mesquite not as a pest to fight, but as a profitable asset to manage for wildlife use and for the production of wood products. Besides wildlife hunting, outdoor wildlife viewing is increasing and has become a multimillion-dollar industry. Proper multiple-use management of rangeland brush, especially mesquite, is essential for optimum rangeland use and profitability.

The Uses of Mesquite

Mesquite has been an essential resource which humankind has tapped for a myriad of uses throughout recorded history. From the earliest uses of mesquite for food, shelter, and medicine to our modern uses in furniture, flooring, and cooking wood, mesquite has played an integral role in the lives of humans. Current interest in mesquite's ability to withstand severe drought while facilitating the addition of nitrogen and organic matter to the soil, its pod's attractiveness as a food source, its use as an ornamental landscape specimen, and its incorporation into a multitude of wood and food products will ensure mesquite's position as one of the Southwest's most promising natural resources for many years.

Use of Mesquite by the Southwestern Indians

Mesquite was integral in most all aspects of the lives of the southwestern Indians. It was a partner in everyday life and a reliable friend in times when food was extremely scarce during periodic long-term droughts.

Mesquite beans were one of the most important, if not the most important, food staples for many of these Indians. Throughout the southwestern United States they gathered millions of pounds of pods annually; in years of food shortages mesquite beans were often the only food source available.

Mesquite was used for barter between the early Pima and Apache tribes. When food plants failed during droughts in their lands, the Pima took distant journeys into Apache country to obtain food. In exchange for articles brought by the Pima the Apache gave them mesquite beans and bean meal.

Most of the early Indian tribes employed a nearly universal procedure to prepare the mesquite for eating. The beans were prepared by pounding with a stone mortar and pestle or with a large wooden pole for large quantities. The pods were ground with the seeds or the extremely hard seeds were parched separately by tossing them up in a basket of live coals then ground into a meal. Indian women lined bas-

"Valiant Warrior." (Photo © Charlie Boren, master wood sculptor, Burleson, Texas)

kets with clean hides, on which were placed successive layers of crushed pods and beans; each layer was sprinkled with water and allowed to stand overnight. When dry, the mass caked together so densely that it could be kept for an indefinite period without appreciable spoilage. Throughout the cold winter months when fresh food was not readily available, this "cake" was eaten without further preparation and considered a great delicacy. When stored for any length of time, it became a living dynamic mass, upon generations of beetles that originally were present in the seeds feeding on it. To many tribes, including the Pima, this made little difference: the beetles were not removed but accepted as an agreeable ingredient. When pulverized to a flour, the bean and beetle mixture became a homogeneous mass of animal and vegetable matter. The Pima made dough out of the flour and cooked it as round cakes. Certain tribes such as the Pima and Opata also made a kind of effervescent beer from the beans, preparing an atole by mixing flour with water that readily underwent fermentation.

Mesquite gum extracted from wounds on the tree was also widely utilized by many Indian tribes. It was used to color pottery before it was fired in their cooking fires. Mesquite gum and clay mixtures were spread on the head to cure lice infestations. Mesquite gum, leaves, roots, and bark were used in many other medicinal preparations. Aqueous solutions of gum and leaves were utilized to treat eye ailments, skin disorders, diarrhea and stomach complaints, and excessive menses. Gum dissolved in hot water was a common gargle for throat infections.

Mesquite gum was a vital and important element in many mystical and religious ceremonies. A Pima warrior, after killing an Apache, underwent a cleansing ceremony of sixteen days; his head was plastered with mud and mesquite gum, which was allowed to remain for eight of the days. Many other rituals surrounded the mesquite tree. When a Yuma girl reached puberty, her mother prepared a plaster of mesquite gum and clay which the young woman placed on the head of any man who came to her home during the puberty ceremony; the man left the ointment on his head overnight to create a mystical bond with the young woman. The mother then plastered the young woman's hair with the mixture, which was allowed to remain on her head until the next day, consummating the bond.

In a chapter in the book *Ethnic Medicines in the Southwest* entitled "Disease and Curing in a Yaqui Community," Mary Elizabeth Shutler states that the Yaqui Indians of Sonora, Mexico, still hold many mythological beliefs in which plants and animals play a vital role, passed down through hundreds of years. The Yaqui believe that a supernatural power which they call seataka is inherent in the animals and plants of the wilderness. One of the five cures for illness, seataka is an archaic Yaqui word of rather obscure meaning, literally translated "flower-body." It is the innate and mysterious power possessed by an individual that gives curing powers and the knowledge of which plants could cure. Seataka also exists in the plants and rocks of the monte, the Yaqui term for any wild place. Two plants in particular have supernatural powers beyond the natural powers of plants to nourish or cure, the hu'upa or mesquite and the hiyakvivam or tobacco. Only the hu'upa, which grows in sacred Yaqui territory, has mysterious curing powers to detect and vanquish witchcraft, especially if the wood is cut in the shape of a cross. One Yaqui myth tells of a "talking stick" of mesquite wood which foretold death to all people baptized as Christians. According to this story, Christ came to Sonora while the Yaqui wandered about, hunting and growing their foods. Those who wished to be baptized burned the stick and those who wished to remain unbaptized became enchanted and went to live, undying and invisible, in the monte.

Mesquite was such an omnipresent and nutritious resource and central part of life itself that many tribes such as the Walapai, Apache, Papago, and Maricopa honored mesquite in their language and mythology. The creation myth of the Maricopa states that the Maricopa, Pima, and Yavapai, after the death of their maker, scattered over the country and gathered mesquite beans. An Apache myth recounts how the sun and the moon consulted together and then formed a mesquite tree and hung bunches of beans upon its branches. The death of the coyote myth of the Pima tells of mesquite surviving the great flood and of how the coyote ate so many mesquite beans that they swelled up in his stomach, causing his death.

Mesquite also played a role in many southwestern Indians' entertainment and leisure times. One of the most important of the Papago games was a footrace in which a ball, usually made of mesquite wood or mesquite gum about the size of a croquet ball, was kicked along by each contestant. The Pima played a game known as kits, very similar to field hockey, using mesquite sticks. The Maricopa Indians hit a roughly shaped ball made from mesquite in another competitive game very similar to our modern field hockey.

Mesquite wood barbecuing of meats and vegetables is a very popular pastime today. Southwest Indians also preferred mesquite for many of the same reasons: it burns with intense heat, is readily available, and imparts a rich deep smoke flavor to meats. Rotten mesquite wood was the preferred wood of the Kamia Indians. Due to its high heat content, a mesquite fire also was used for firing their pottery to increase its durability.

Many Indian tribes used mesquite as a fiber. The Cocopa women made baskets from mesquite roots, while the Yuma inserted the binding willows of their coiled basketry with a small pointed mesquite stick. Mesquite bark fiber dyed black by soaking for four days in water containing black mesquite-bark gum was used in warriors' girdles. Cordage among the Seri was commonly made of mesquite root fiber and was used for making bowstrings, harpoon cords, balsas, and fabrics.

A musical instrument used in the Corn Festival of the Pima and Maricopa consisted of three flattish mesquite baskets spread with a layer of mesquite gum. When rubbed with a bone, these baskets produced a sound resembling a squawk or shriek.

Mesquite played an important role in construction. Many stavelike ribs of mesquite were tied to horizontal poles to form load-bearing walls of early Pima dwellings; the roof timbers were also often mesquite. Mesquite was frequently the wood of choice for rough furniture due to its durability and strength, the same characteristics desired by

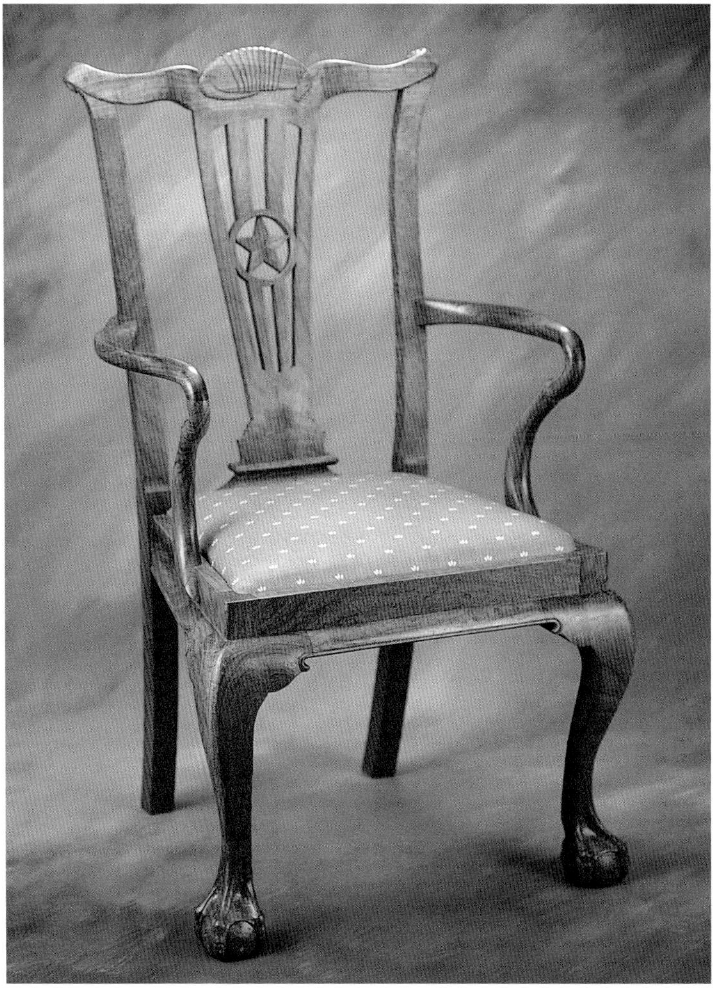

Many exquisite woodworks, such as this chair crafted by Leslie Mizell of Cleveland, Texas, are made from mesquite by some of the finest craftspersons in the United States. (Photo © Leslie Mizell, Cleveland, Texas)

woodworkers today. A Yuma baby cradle was made by the father immediately after birth of his child by using a slender length of mesquite wood bent to a long U-shape on which flat transverse slats were lashed. The hoops of mesquite were curved over the upper end as a frame for an awning. This same form of mesquite cradle was found among the Mohave and Pima.

Weapons and agricultural implements were also made from mesquite. Yuma used mesquite to make war clubs and spears or "stabbing sticks" sharpened on one end and hardened with fire. In much of the Southwest mesquite made the best bow wood, but clear, straight lengths were hard to find. Two simple agricultural tools of the Yuma were the weed cutter and the planter, or dibble, both often made from mesquite wood. The Seri used mesquite wood to construct the main shaft of their turtle harpoons and the roots to form the end poles of their fish nets.

Mesquite played a major role in the lives of early cultures far back in recorded history. It was an inherent and trusted partner in humankind's march through time. It supplied many of life's daily necessities and held a spiritual, mystical, and sacred position.

Characteristics of Mesquite Wood

In the early history of the southwestern United States mesquite played a vital role in supplying a wealth of items such as wagon wheels, food, medicines, weapons, and even paving blocks for early streets in many major population centers. Many of these applications were adopted by western settlers from the Southwest Indians, who used mesquite for centuries before early western settlement days.

Mesquite is one of the most remarkable woods in North America. Its beauty and working properties rival those of other fine hardwoods such as oak, walnut, and cherry. With its swirling grain, variable color, and occasional character defects—such as ingrown bark, mineral streaks, bug blemishes, and latent buds—mesquite offers a hidden treasure for the woodworker intent on creating exquisite furniture, flooring, and other woodwork.

Mesquite wood is medium to coarse in texture, with the grain being quite irregular, often interlocking. The wood is easy to work, finishes smoothly, and takes a high natural sheen when polished. When dried it is extremely stable and quite resistant to both decay and insect attack.

Mesquite's sapwood, the wood that is closest to the bark, is pale yellowish-white in color and is about one-half to one inch wide regardless of tree size and age. Its heartwood, the darker wood in the center of the tree, ranges from a dark yellowish-brown through shades of gray-brown to deep reddish, almost purple-brown. Age produces a distinct patina—as the heartwood is exposed to ultraviolet light, its color changes to a uniform warm dark brown, despite its original color.

Mesquite wood has many very attractive physical and mechanical properties for woodworking. Wood, unlike other construction materials such as plastic and steel, has different physical properties in three distinct cellular directions—radially (from the pith to the bark, perpendicular to the growth rings), tangentially (tangent to the growth rings, parallel to the growth rings), and longitudinally (up and down the tree). A wood's dimensional stability (its shrinkage or swelling in response to the exposure to changes in moisture conditions) is of great concern in woodworking applications such as furniture and flooring. The amount of shrinkage and swelling will depend on how the wood is cut from the tree—most commercial woods swell two to three times more in the tangential direction than in the radial direction, with very little change in the longitudinal direction. For example, when exposed to water or high humidity, black walnut wood swells 3.3 and 8.7 percent in the radial and tangential directions, respectively. If subjected to moisture, black walnut wood in furniture or in a floor could incur severe warpage due to its differential swelling. In contrast, when subjected to the same moisture, mesquite will swell equally in the radial and tangential directions, 2.2 and 2.6 percent, respectively, resulting in very little distortion. In other words, mesquite wood cut into a square will stay a square, even when exposed to severe moisture conditions. When cut from almost any other wood, the square will become an irregular polygon. This gives mesquite a tremendous advantage over other woods in products such as furniture and flooring and also explains why turnings and carvings can be produced from relatively green mesquite wood and dried slowly with minor shrinkage problems.

Anatomically speaking, mesquite wood is a diffuse, porous hardwood with variable-width growth rings. When the end-grain of a piece

Table 6. Selected Physical and Mechanical Properties of Mesquite Wood in Comparison to Other Fine Woods

Species	Density (lbs./ft.^{2})	Radial/ Tangential (volumetric shrinkage) (%)	Side Hardness (lbs.)	Bending Strength (million lbs./in.^{2})
Mesquite	45.0	2.2 / 2.6 (4.7)	2,336	1.38
Southern Red Oak	36.8	4.7 / 11.3 (16.1)	1,060	1.49
Hard Maple	39.3	4.8 / 9.9 (14.7)	1,450	1.62
Black Walnut	24.3	3.3 / 8.7 (13.9)	1,010	1.68
Teak	34.3	2.5 / 5.8 (8.7)	1,000	1.55
Honduras Mahogany	30.2	3.0 / 4.1 (7.2)	800	1.50
Brazilian Rosewood	49.9	2.9 / 4.6 (7.6)	2,720	1.88
Purpleheart	41.8	3.2 / 6.1 (9.5)	1,860	2.27

Source: Rogers 1986.

of mesquite wood is observed under a 10x hand lens, it can be seen that each pore is surrounded by smaller cells called parenchyma. Parenchyma cells most noticeably define the mesquite's growth rings.

Much of mesquite's highly figured, variable wood grain is caused by unique growing factors and conditions. Dormant buds in the wood just under the bark give some mesquite wood the traditional "bird's eye" figure. These dormant buds never begin growing unless the tree is injured or cut down, when they sprout from the stump profusely. Burls, which are abnormal swellings of a limb or the bole caused by the attack of insects, disease, or mistletoe disrupting the tree's growth, also provide highly figured wood that is much prized. Other mesquite wood that is much sought after is found in the limb crotches or forks in the tree's crown. At a crotch wood tissues from two or more limbs blend together, resulting in unique "crotch figures" or "crotch-wood," greatly valued by woodworkers. Much of the most highly figured wood of any tree is found in these crotches.

Rootwood is noticeably harder and more figured than "normal" stemwood. Swirling grain can be found at and just below the mesquite's root collar at the ground line. Many woodworkers in the southwestern United States travel to recently bulldozed rangeland to collect rootwood

Table 7. Location of Highly Figured Wood in Mesquite Trees

- Limb and bole forks and crotches
- Rootwood (especially at the root collar at the ground line)
- Insect and disease burls (swellings)
- Mistletoe burls (swellings)
- Locations with excessive dormant buds
- Wood under blemishes or injuries on the bark surface
- Wood from the bole of a tree with spiral grain

from the stumps and carry it back to their shop, where the root sections are sliced into slabs, dried, and then crafted into exquisite items such as tabletops, desktops, and floors.

Mesquite wood is quite heavy—green mesquite wood weighs about forty-six pounds per cubic foot, a specific gravity of 0.75, about that of the hard oaks. Its bending and hardness strength is equal or superior to that of competitive woods such as red oak, black walnut, and hard maple. Table 6 illustrates mesquite's exceptional properties.

Mesquite wood, like all woods, is composed of three basic chemical constituents: long-chain, carbon-based cellulose that is the building block of the wood structure, lignin or wood glues that keep the wood together, and extractives that give each type of wood its distinctive color, flavor, and smell and influence many of its chemical, mechanical, and physical properties. Mesquite has an unusually high extractive content of around 14 percent, the extractive content of most common hardwoods being around 5 or 6 percent. A high extractive content contributes to mesquite's extremely high dimensional stability and its attractive wood-smoke flavor during barbecuing. Extractives can also

Table 8. Chemical Analysis of Mesquite Wood

CONSTITUENT	PERCENTAGE
Ash content	0.5
Extractive content	14.0
Cellulose	57.5
Lignin	28.0

Source: D. Adams 1968.

A Mesquite Profile: Master Sculptor Charlie Boren, Burleson, Texas

Charlie Boren's watchword for his mesquite sculpture could easily be "one man's waste is another's treasure," as he looks at old, rough, weather-beaten sections of waste wood and sees exquisite eagles, fantastic Indian shamans, and swirling dolphins that others fail to see.

His works of beauty can be seen at many art shows and exhibits across Texas, such as the State Fair of Texas and the Cottonwood Art Festival in North Dallas. A collection of twenty-eight of his natural wood sculptures recently toured the southwestern United States, showing in many museums and art galleries.

Working from his studio in Burleson, Texas, Charlie Boren is one of a limited number of full-time commercial, professional wood sulptors in the United States who create fine masterpieces from large, rough pieces of wood. "Much of my wood is collected in and around central Texas's Lake Buchanan, wood that has drifted down creeks and dry washes during the floods that occur in the Hill Country. Nature does the harvesting and also the drying. When I find those unique pieces, they go back to my studio. There I study each piece to see what is it that I should make from it." Viewing Charlie's masterful sculptures, one sees a grand compilation of the inner feelings and essence of the creator. Created by his genius, these sculptures leave the viewer with a feeling at the deep, alluring beauty of nature at its best.

Using many of Texas's native woods such as mesquite, ash, hackberry, pecan, cedar, and oak, Charlie creates masterpieces from gnarled, twisted, and misshapen sections of dry wood collected from a local lake-side ranch near Buchanan Dam, Texas. Mesquite is his wood of choice for carving Southwest Indians, eagles, swans, egrets, mountain men, and many other themes.

The theme of each sculpture comes from the rough wood itself, which generates expressions of what it should be. "You don't just pick up a piece and begin to carve a bird. You look the wood over, studying it in detail, and keep turning it over and over. Like a light being turned on, something pricks the mind and the piece will not just be a bird, but a majestic eagle." In that fashion Charlie has carved profesionally for the past twenty-five years. His love of carving comes from his early childhood days of sitting on the porch watching an old friend telling stories of early Texas, reliving times of old. "While the yarns were told, Uncle Gene's hands were whittling the small prairie critters he knew from days gone by. He gave me my first knife and at his side I learned to love the shape and feel of these small sculptures! His words made pictures in my mind, while his hands, big and strong, whittled... and I watch the whittling." After a time in the education profession as a teacher and coach, Charlie made a decision to try his lot with his first love, as a professional sculptor. He has never looked back. Charlie combines an uncanny ability to "see into the wood itself" with perseverance to bring out the ultimate splendor of the ordinary, which the common viewer cannot see.

But, as with most talent, inherent abilities have to be cultivated. In the past years Charlie has studied under some of the European masters of sculpture, making trips to Oberammergau, Germany; Cheltenham, England; and St. Jean Port Joli, Quebec, Canada. At each point in the continuum of the artistic life, the artist appreciates or understands better or reaches a deeper awareness of his relationship to his medium. "The most gratifying reward that an artist can receive is seeing patrons truly receiving delight from his work. As with all art, sculpture is meant to be enjoyed. If the viewer goes away with a sense of pleasure, of passion for what the artist is trying to portray, a state of bliss, then sincerely the artist indeed has succeeded in his pursuit."

cause the woodworker grief: they gum up saws, making a wood harder to cut and often causing overheating of saw blades.

Mesquite Woodworking

Mesquite is one of the world's best woods, uniquely suitable for fine woodwork, especially for furniture and flooring. Its mechanical and physical properties give exceptional strength, performance, and beauty, while its deep, rich colors, when mixed with natural grain and character marks, result in a floor seldom matched in the industry.

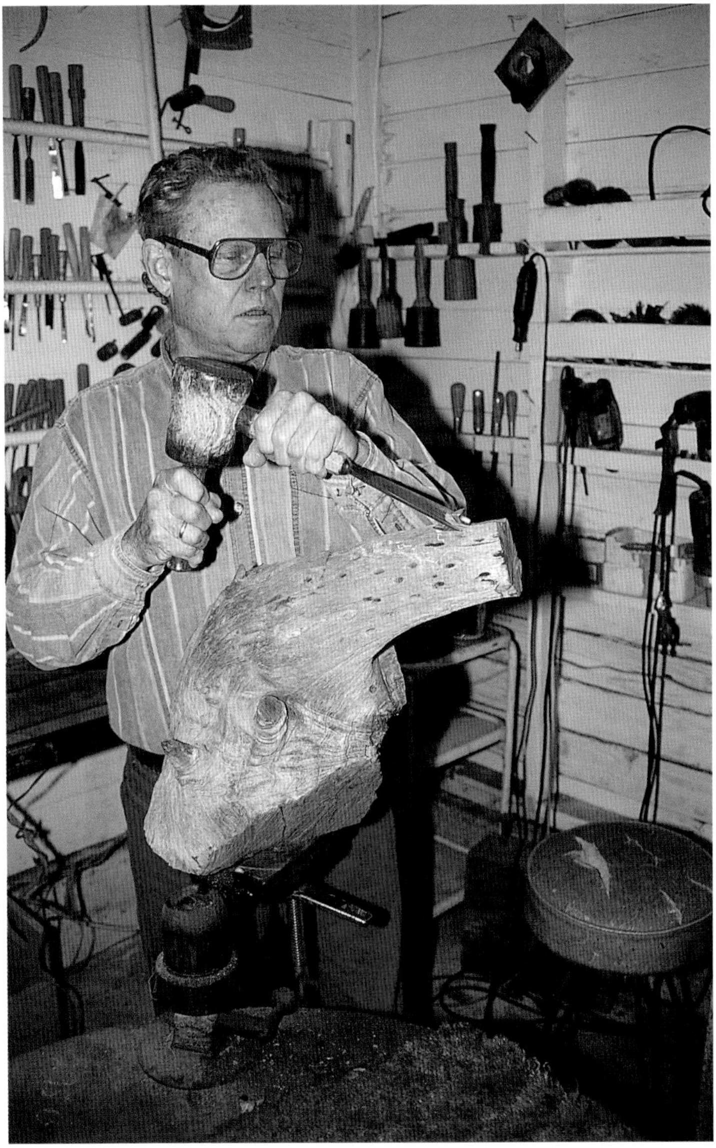

Charlie Boren makes extensive use of the old way of hand carving in his exquisite eagles, Indians, and abstract sculptures.
(Photo © Ken E. Rogers)

Mesquite lumber is unlike that cut from oak, walnut, and ash timber in the eastern United States, which is reasonably clear of defects and available in large dimensions. Mesquite lumber is usually short (four to six feet) and narrow (four to six inches), although larger dimensions can be obtained. A clear board six inches wide and six feet long is extremely unusual. In spite of the scarcity of large, clear boards, most mesquite lumber can be incorporated into furniture, flooring, or other woodwork by using their defects in the design to add beauty and uniqueness.

Homeowners who want to have mesquite flooring but want to save money or install their own floors can do so. Mesquite floor installation is not difficult technically, but it is a very tedious, back-breaking job. Hours and hours are spent on the floor installing the floor piece by piece. Little experience is necessary; the procedures are cookbook. Homeowners can contact a mesquite flooring mill, purchase the square footage of flooring required, and quite easily, but with care, install their own beautiful mesquite floor.

Due to its great dimensional stability, mesquite wood is easily dried. Wood must be dried from the fresh condition of about 50 percent moisture content called the green state to a moisture content that it will be exposed to during use in a home or other location. After it is installed, mesquite wood's moisture content equalizes with the humidity of the location, to about 8 to 12 percent in the southwestern United States. In spite of its ease of drying, mesquite wood still requires drying at the proper temperature and humidity to avoid defects such as splitting, warping, and cupping. There are three basic steps: drying the wood to the appropriate moisture content that it will reach after it is put in use, equalizing all of the pieces of wood to the same moisture content, and conditioning the wood at a high temperature and high humidity for a short period to relieve physical stresses that develop in the wood during drying. Each step must be properly completed to produce quality wood for woodworking. If not, problems of warping, cupping, or splitting will mysteriously show up, either immediately or in the finished piece of woodwork sometime in the future.

Mesquite's dimensional stability and its ease of drying are very attractive, especially to wood turners and sculptors who work with large blocks of wood that normally give them problems when dried. Craftspersons will be delighted the first time they "work" mesquite

Table 9. Mesquite Lumber Drying Schedule

MOISTURE CONTENT AT START	LUMBER THICKNESS 1", 1¼", 1½"		LUMBER THICKNESS 2" AND THICKER	
%	Temperature (° F)	Humidity (%)	Temperature (° F)	Humidity (%)
>40	120	7	110	5
40	120	10	110	7
35	120	15	110	10
30	130	25	120	19
25	140	35	130	35
20	150	40	140	40
15	180	50	160	50
Equalizing (2 or 3 hours' duration)	173	43	173	43
Equalizing (2 or 3 hours' duration)	180	10	180	10

Source: Rogers 1993.

semidried and realize that it does not distort, split, or crack when it eventually dries. Many wood turners in Texas work mesquite semigreen, finish the work on the wood lathe, and then allow their work to dry slowly without difficulty.

Using mesquite in woodworking quickly reveals that the wood is extremely variable in its properties. One piece will shrink little when dried, then the next will really split, warp, and distort. One piece will be extremely hard, while the next may be excessively soft. The reason for this is that mesquite grows on sites with extremes of conditions and environments. Dry and wet sites affect growth—the drier the site, the slower the growth. Moist, wet, deep, and fertile bottomland sites will cause mesquite to grow extremely fast, giving it wider annual growth rings, softer, weaker, and looser-looking grain, and lighter-weight wood. Dry, infertile, shallow, rocky, upland soils slow mesquite's

Table 10. Variation in the Physical and Mechanical Properties of Mesquite (Prosopis glandulosa *var.* glandulosa)

PROPERTY	LOWEST	HIGHEST	COMMONLY USED VALUE	AVERAGE PERCENT DEVIATION
Density (lbs./ft.^{3})	39.9	61.6	45.0	54.4
Bending Strength (lbs.)	612,000	1,441,000	1,380,000	136
Volumetric Shrinkage (%)	1.8	7.5	4.7	316.7
Side Hardness (lbs.)	1,210	3,010	2,336	149

Source: Rogers 1986.

growth, resulting in narrow annual rings, hard, tighter-looking grain, and much heavier wood. No other application reveals this more than flooring, where denser, harder wood will wear really well and the lighter-weight, softer wood will not withstand the wear and tear of continuous walking. Flooring manufacturers need to be conscious of mesquite's extremely variable weight and softness. Soft, fast-growing mesquite will not hold up to heavy traffic in applications like building lobbies, restaurants, and doorways. Slower-growing mesquite, identified by close growth rings and heavier weight, will be best for these applications. With proper wood selection, a floor manufactured from mesquite can have a service life of fifty years or more.

When making various mesquite wood products, many woodworkers have their own special glues and wood finishes that they swear are the best for mesquite. Standard yellow wood glue and the two-part

A Mesquite Profile:
"The World Famous Mesquite Rocker"
Robert Hensarling, Uvalde, Texas

Deep in the south Texas brush country a man struggles with a log of mesquite, wrestling it onto his sixteen-foot trailer. This is repeated with a determined regularity until a goodly number of logs are cut and harvested. The beginning of a great transformation has begun. This transformation, like unto a miracle from God, comes from the hands of a single man, Robert Hensarling, master woodcrafter and furniture maker. Hensarling transforms these gnarled, twisted mesquite logs into a beautiful art object, his exquisite rocking chair, known widely as the "Maloof Mesquite Rocker."

Hensarling crafts his rocker almost completely from mesquite, often with accents added from another favorite south Texas wood, the Texas ebony, revealing his deep love of mesquite and his deep love of woodworking. Hensarling says, "It's a lot of work, taking over two hundred hours for each chair to form," he signs each under the left arm because he is left-handed. "I work fourteen hours a day six days a week and seven hours on the seventh. I'm not getting rich, but I'm making a living doing what I love." He is presently on chair number 156; his rocker has evolved through a number of transformations from a straight back, square form, to the current free-flowing rocker that seems to fit a person perfectly, modeled after the world-renowned walnut rocking chair of his mentor, Sam Maloof of California. "Studying under Mr. Maloof in furniture classes through the years has inspired me so that I named my rocker after him—the Maloof Mesquite Rocker." Hensarling and his rockers have been highlighted in periodicals such as the *Wall Street Journal* and *USA Today*, as well as on regional TV shows as "The Eyes of Texas" and "Texas Country Reporter."

But Hensarling's Maloof Mesquite Rocker may not be his greatest claim to fame or his most impressive piece of woodwork. "In 1995, a New York City businessman walked into his shop and, after seeing my rocker, immediately asked me to have a conference table made from mesquite for his south Texas home he was currently building." After all was said and done, or rather cut and sanded, Robert came up with the design and the manufacture of a twenty-foot, six-pedestal conference table with sixteen matching, straight-back, "Maloof-style" chairs. The table itself weighed over 1,000 pounds. "The table is the single largest piece of mesquite furniture that I have ever heard of," says Hensarling. "It took over eight months to build, from the tree, to the sawmill, and then to the dry kiln and eventually into the finished table and chairs; it was quite a job."

But things weren't always "big-time" for Robert. Fifteen years ago, after leaving the Uvalde police department, as a struggling woodworker he survived by making thousands of cutting boards and boxes from mesquite. He progressed into making and laying mesquite flooring but quickly found that was not true woodworking, not really creative. He then saw a Sam Maloof walnut rocker in a book and determined that was what he wanted to build.

Woodworking runs deep in Hensarling's blood. His great-grandfather had a sawmill back in Mississippi; when clearcutting left him without timber in the early 1900s, he picked up his family and moved to Madisonville, Texas. Hensarling's father, Bill, followed the family tradition when he built a wood lathe at the age of ten and powered it with a sewing machine treadle. Now

Bill Hensarling is the "chief engineer" on many of Robert's projects, both designing and building various pieces of machinery, including a crane system for moving the New Yorker's massive mesquite conference table.

Hensarling communicated his love of woodworking willingly to anyone who listens. Visitors who come to his shop find him working hard but always ready to share his secrets of woodworking. "Someone once shared theirs with me, and now I'm sharing with others," he explains. Through dogged determination he has approached the pinnacle of the woodworking fraternity, but he is quick to state that the friends he's made along the way are really valuable rewards.

The "Texas mesquite rocker." (Photo © Robert Hensarling, master furniture-maker, Uvalde, Texas)

epoxies are very popular, while lacquer sealers and various polyurethane finishes are the common mesquite wood finishes.

The Mesquite Wood Industry in Texas

According to a survey made in 1995 by the Texas Forest Service, the mesquite industry in Texas includes about 250 persons and small companies operating sawmills, cooking-wood operations, and woodworking enterprises. Probably three-fourths of these are operating on a part-time basis, averaging just a few hours a week or operating full-time only part of the year. Many of these businesses depend on the Christmas gift season for the bulk of their sales and therefore operate at a much more active pace during the months before Christmas shows and other seasonal shows during the fall and winter. Many of these part-timers are retirees, woodworking for pleasure, selling their crafts to support their hobby, or selling their woodwork to generate a part-time income. Other part-timers operate their woodworking business as a supplement to a full-time occupation. Twenty to thirty mesquite enterprises are full-time ongoing businesses that are very active in daily production, marketing, and shipping of their products, often all over the world. These are primarily the lumber, flooring, cooking-wood, and furniture manufacturers, with five to fifty employees each, and many full-time individual sculptors and wood turners. These enterprises usually operate forty to sixty hours per week, fifty-two weeks a year, and process thousands of cords of mesquite annually.

In the mesquite lumber, furniture, and flooring industries the desirable mesquite logs are usually from ten to sixteen inches in diameter and greater than four feet in length. Many factors can lower the quality of a sawlog. Short, small logs can be used but are marginal for sawmilling because they yield less lumber, especially the more valuable longer lengths. Because mesquite trees are usually crooked and short-bodied, long logs are scarce and command a much higher price. Landowners receiving payment for their logs should realize this. Defects in mesquite are very common: most logs contain wind shakes, splits, bark pockets, and borer damage that, although attractive to the viewer, can make a log less valuable to the sawmiller. A crooked log that has more than two or three inches of sweep (measured by stretching a string from the edge of one end of the log to the edge of the other end and measuring the maximum deviation of the string from the log's bark edge) is a much lower-quality sawlog than a straight log. Essentially, a six-foot log that deviates more than two or three inches in sweep is really two three-foot logs or three two-foot logs, at least as far as the sawmiller goes, and is a much lower-quality sawlog or even a reject log.

Standards for mesquite wood purchased by cooking-wood processors are not as stringent as those for sawmillers because their logs will be sawn into inch-thick disks or "lily-pads" then chunked or chipped. Most cooking-wood companies prefer logs about six to ten inches in diameter and at least two feet long. Small logs are easier to process with the typical cutting equipment used and are much easier to handle. Several companies operate their own harvesting crews and have tight control over log quality and dimensions. They harvest large volumes of wood, hauling truckloads of eight or nine cords at a time to the processing site. Others use contract crews or buy their wood on the open market from independent loggers that deliver one to ten cords at a time. To meet the seasonal demands for cooking and smoking wood, many companies keep as little as a few hundred or as much as two thousand or more cords of wood in inventory at any given time. Marketing is primarily done by packaging their own company brand of wood and selling to grocery brokers or large chain supermarket buyers or by selling to independent wholesalers who have their own private label and resell to smaller stores and retail outlets. In 1996 it was estimated that the cooking wood industry processed about 12,000 cords of wood.

In the lumbering business mesquite logs are usually sawn into either one- or two-inch lumber, run through an edger to remove the bark and sapwood edges, end-cut to length, and dried in a dry kiln. As previously mentioned, mesquite wood for furniture, flooring, or craft use needs to be dried to a moisture content of about 8 to 12 percent, about the moisture content it will have during actual use. Generally, sawmills in the mesquite industry are of two types: portable bandsaw mills, which are slow, but cut really fine, smooth lumber and produce a high yield of lumber from each log, and circle saw mills, which use 48- to 60-inch-diameter circle saws that cut at a much faster rate but cut rougher lumber and have lower lumber yields. Each type has its advantages and drawbacks. The average industry-wide yield of usable lumber from a cord of mesquite is about 250 to 300 board feet. Once dried, the lumber is then run through a planer to produce a smooth surface, ready for sale as finished lumber, for flooring, or for conversion into furniture. The ever-present defects in mesquite lumber make it more attractive for some uses such as table tops, wood turnings, bandsawn boxes, or fireplace mantles. In fine wooden items, the defects that contain voids in the wood's surface are usually filled with a plastic clearcoat or epoxy filler to make a really smooth surface. The

Much of the mesquite crafted into fine woodwork originates from small bandsaw mills such as this one located in Uvalde, Texas. (Photo © Ken E. Rogers)

customer is often looking for natural defects and is willing to pay a premium price.

One large-volume wood product manufactured from mesquite is wood flooring. Mesquite makes some of the finest and most durable hardwood flooring available anywhere in the world. Several styles of mesquite flooring are manufactured. One type, side-grain or "flat-sawn" strip flooring, is usually two to three inches wide in random lengths and usually from three-eighths to one-half inch thick. Another type, tongue-and-groove, is a similar-sized, flat-sawn flooring, but it is run through a molding machine that puts a tongue and a groove on the opposite edges of each piece. Tongue-and-groove flooring is a standard in the hardwood flooring business, and the availability of tongue-and-groove mesquite flooring has made mesquite a more acceptable "off-the-shelf product" to many flooring wholesalers, interior designers, and architects. A third style of flooring manufactured from mesquite is "end-grain" flooring, which is made by slicing the log or large lumber perpendicular to the grain into three-eighth to half-inch-thick pieces. Thus the floor's surface is the wood's end-grain surface, which is more than 50 percent harder than the side grain surface. Also, manufacturing yields of end-grain flooring are greater, and it dries much faster and more easily than strip flooring (end-grain wood dries 100 times faster than side-grain wood).

Many methods of drying lumber and flooring are used in the mesquite industry—solar, vacuum, dehumidification, direct wood fired, and accelerated air-drying being a few. Each has its own characteristics, drying time, and other unique features.

To be successful in marketing mesquite wood products such as flooring, furniture, crafts, sculptures, and lumber, craftspersons need to approach marketing as a creative, multifaceted enterprise. What works for one person and product may not work for another. Due to low sawmilling yields and high labor requirements coupled with mesquite's beauty and in-service performance, mesquite products command a much higher price than comparable walnut, oak, or cherry wood products, often two to three times or more. Mesquite marketers do not have traditional established channels of sales and promotion. Each producer has to develop and aggressively build these channels for his or her own product line. Successful mesquite producers have used many marketing angles, depending on their particular product and the re-

Tough as nails, mesquite wood makes some of the finest parquet flooring in the world, as can be seen in the Hilton Palacio del Rio Hotel in San Antonio. (Photo © Ken E. Rogers of the mesquite floor in the lobby of the Hilton Palacio del Rio Hotel, 200 South Alamo Street, San Antonio, Texas)

Typical Mesquite Floor Installation

Select quality mesquite wood that is hard, with a tight grain, relatively free of defects, of even thickness, and with the proper moisture content. Assemble the necessary tools: straight edge, floor sander, sandpaper, mastic, and wood finish.

1. Use a straightedge to level the floor, grinding down the high spots. Fill using a latex milk filler, applying it only about ¼ inch thick at the time.

2. Lay out the floor with a string line and place the mesquite pieces straight down into the mastic adhesive. Do not apply a piece and move it over to align, as the mastic will slowly move your pieces back to the original spot.

3. Wait 24 hours then roll with a 150-pound roller or step on each piece a time or two. Allow 1 week to dry.

4. Using a good drum sander, sand the floor, beginning with a #4 or #16 grit and proceeding to fine grits of #36, #60, and #100. Use a wet tack cloth between grits. On the last pass with each grit, go with the grain on flat-sawn flooring.

5. After the #36 grit, fill the cracks with a paste such as Glitsa. Mix it with fine mesquite sander dust to give it mesquite's color. Trowel it into the cracks. On small jobs, use a wood putty, mixing cherry with walnut colors to match the mesquite.

6. Sand after filling with #100 grit.

7. Use an oil-modified polyurethane finish such as Duraseal semi-gloss. Apply four coats of finish. After each coat; let dry 24 hours and hand sand with #150 grit burnished paper, cleaning with a tack cloth between sandings. Spot fill between coats with filler.

8. Maintain a good wax on the floor. It should be refinished every few years when necessary.

sources available. Buyer trade shows, interior design and architectural shows, woodworking and craft shows, wholesale sales to retail gift shops, sales directly to woodworking guilds and clubs, wholesale gift shows, and direct sales via mail order and magazine advertisements are just a few marketing and promotion channels used by successful mesquite entrepreneurs. It is important to have a quality product in inventory and a quality brochure and to market aggressively. In the words of David Miller of Bastrop, Texas, who has been marketing fine mesquite products for over a decade, the key is to "contact the right person with cash, and the desire to have a unique product, a mesquite product!"

Mesquite's Biomass Energy Feedstock Potential

Mesquite wood has been considered a potential raw material for energy production for more than twenty years. In a study done by the Texas Forest Products Laboratory in the early 1980s, it was determined that mesquite rangelands could supply enough raw material for a 60,000-pound-per-hour steam boiler using the mesquite grown in a radius of ten miles of the boiler site. Other studies including one investigation at Texas A&M University at Kingsville (TAMUK) determined that a 500-megawatt electrical generating plant could be supplied perpetually from the mesquite harvested from within a fourteen-mile radius of the power generation site. At Kingsville research is continuing on the development of a mechanical, portable flail shredding harvester that will sever, shred, collect, and transport small-diameter mesquite wood for use as a biomass feedstock. Although the harvester has successfully harvested brush at a rate of 1 to 2½ acres per hour, much design and biomass marketing analysis will be necessary before it becomes commercially viable.

Although the use of mesquite for biomass energy feedstock is technically feasible, two obstacles exist: harvesting costs are too high, and the density of mesquite brush on Texas rangelands is too low. Until the costs of alternative energies such as fuel oil and natural gas rise significantly or lower-cost harvesting methods are developed, there is small probability that mesquite will be used in the near-term future either for electrical power generation or for feeding a wood-fired boiler generating steam.

Mesquite as an Ornamental Landscape Specimen Tree

Today many people in the southwestern United States are very conscious of the use and availability of water for watering lawns, flowers, and trees. During these times of water shortages and legal restrictions on watering times and water consumption, many homeowners and managers of commercial gardens and golf courses are replanting with native trees that do not need much water. Mesquite is a very attractive tree that meets this criterion and is being used as an ornamental in the southwestern United States and elsewhere worldwide.

Mesquite is used extensively in the southwestern United States as a native ornamental tree, as seen here on the golf course located on the campus of Texas A&M University in College Station.
(Photo © Ken E. Rogers)

Table 11. Mesquites Used in Ornamental Plantings throughout the Southwestern United States

SPECIES	MATURE SIZE (HEIGHT/ SPREAD IN FEET)	FLOWER	HARDINESS (° F)	THORNS	FOLIAGE	PODS
Honey Mesquite *(Prosopis glandulosa)*	20 to 40/ 20 to 40	yellow spikes	-10	yes	green	straight, without visible beading
Chilean Mesquite *(Prosopis chilensis)*	20 to 40/ 20 to 40	light cream-yellow fuzzy spikes	10 to 15	no	dark green	broad, straight or arched, beaded
Screwbean Mesquite *(Prosopis pubescens)*	10 to 20/ 10 to 20	yellow spikes	0	yes	gray-green	smooth, numerous coils (cork-screwed)
Velvet Mesquite *(Prosopis velutina)*	30 to 40/ 30 to 40	green to yellow fuzzy spikes	5	yes	gray-green	straight, beaded
Argentinian Mesquite *(Prosopis alba)*	20 to 40/ 20 to 40	light yellow spikes	10 to 15	yes, but often very few	dark green	straight or slightly curved, beaded and flattened

Several mesquite species have been planted for many years as ornamental landscape specimen trees. Honey mesquite *(Prosopis glandulosa)* and screwbean mesquite *(Prosopis pubescens)* are lovely small trees that fit well into the average landscape, needing minimum care. Honey mesquite has clusters of beautiful, long yellow flowers and is cold hardy to about -10° F. Screwbean mesquite is much smaller, ten to twenty feet tall, with unique very tightly corkscrewed fruit that is very attractive, and is temperature tolerant to about 0° F. Two fast-growing, thornless clones of South American mesquites from Chile and Argentina are becoming the most popular landscape trees in low- and middle-elevation deserts of Texas and California. The Chilean mesquite *Prosopis chilensis*, or white mesquite, reaches heights of twenty to forty feet, whereas the Argentinian *Prosopis alba* is about ten feet taller. Both are cold hardy to about 10 to 15° F.

The most characteristic feature of mesquite that makes it ideal as a landscape plant for arid regions of the world is its ability to withstand drought and to reach down deep to tap the water table. Roots of mesquite spread deep and wide into the soil. Being deep-rooted gives mesquite the ability to "search out" available moisture, a distinctive advantage over many competing plants whose roots do not penetrate the soil as deeply. Also, as previously mentioned, mesquite has the capacity to increase its resistance to water loss as drought conditions increase by drastically reducing its rate of transpiration loss by closing the stomata or pores on its leaflets and by drawing tightly held water from the soil when necessary.

Mesquite's use as an ornamental landscape specimen has several disadvantages, however. Thorns are the main negative characteristic of mesquite. They create a risk for children playing around mesquite, and care must be taken during pruning and maintenance to remove fallen twigs and limbs. Mesquite has two other disadvantages: it drops its leaves in the winter, and its bean pods drop and litter the ground, leaving a large cleanup chore.

The Mesquite Barbecue Wood Industry in the United States

Mesquite wood has been used for outdoor cooking and smoking for many years, but since the early 1980s mesquite has really taken off and become the wood of choice for hundreds of thousands of barbecue enthusiasts throughout the United States and the world.

The most appealing barbecuing characteristics of mesquite wood are the exquisite wood-smoke flavor that it imparts to meats, its high-temperature cooking, and its superiority in "coaling" in the fire bed; it excels in each of these areas when compared with all other cooking woods. Mesquite wood-smoke has a very distinctive odor venerated for many years, as illustrated by J. Frank Dobie's writings in *Arizona Highways* in November 1941:

> I get homesick sometimes for the smell of burning mesquite wood. Many a time in the brush country I have smelled out a Mexican jacal (cabin) hidden by darkness or the lay of the land, by the aroma of mesquite smoke going up its chimney. A friend of mine who often camps in the mesquite country always holds his hands in the smoke every little while during the breakfast period so that they will smell of burning mesquite all the rest of the morning. "For hours afterwards," he says, "I can enjoy the odor of my hands." (Dobie 1941a, 4)

Mesquite wood burning in a fireplace or in an open fire in winter time, in addition to supplying warmth and the light and cheerfulness emanating from all open fires, offers a bouquet of odors. Boyce House, a southwestern writer and poet, describes wood-smoke in very vivid terms in his poem "The Mesquite": "The aroma of the coffee and of the wood-smoke is very sweet— (there is no other smoke like it in the world)."

Backyard barbecue connoisseurs' demand for this wood-smoke aroma has generated a completely new industry, primarily in Texas—marketing mesquite wood products for home cooking and smoking. In the barbecue industry mesquite trees are harvested and reduced to mini-logs, nugget-sized chunks, or chips. Once the material is processed and dried, it is packed in one- to fifty-pound bags and sold to grocery retailers, food supply brokers, and restaurants or directly to the user. Demand for this "golden mesquite" wood has increased from a small cottage industry in the early 1980s in Texas, Arizona, and New Mexico to an industry that processed more than fifty million pounds of wood in 1996.

The reputation of mesquite wood for barbecuing has spread worldwide, and wood processed in Texas is exported to many overseas locations such as Europe and the Far East. One company exports mesquite cooking wood to the far reaches of the earth through the United States Armed Forces Exchanges. Connoisseurs of fine barbecuing throughout the world never have to be without their favorite wood—mesquite.

Mesquite's high extractive content, the same quality that gives the wood its very high dimensional stability in wood product applications, is the "secret ingredient" that produces its rich, distinctive smoke aroma.

Millions of pounds of mesquite cooking chips and chunks are processed and shipped to many locations worldwide. (Photo © Ken E. Rogers)

Consumer surveys through the years have ranked mesquite equal to or superior to other competitive cooking woods such as hickory, fruitwood, grapevine, and alder.

The mesquite cooking-wood industry utilizes a high percentage of the trees it harvests—almost all the above-ground portions. Usually all limbs more than two inches in diameter are cut and harvested, with stems less than two inches in diameter and the leaves left on the site, contributing nutrients and organic matter for soil fertility. Dead or dying trees are the preferred resource for cooking wood, as they require less energy during drying.

During processing the sawdust produced in the milling operation is dried and sized and sold to the commercial meat-smoking industry, the charcoal briquette industry, or the liquid smoke industry. Commercial meat smokers use the mesquite sawdust in their wood burners, infusing their meats slowly with mesquite's sweet smoke.

Large volumes of mesquite sawdust are incorporated into charcoal briquettes. Large briquette manufacturers combine clay, charcoal from wood or coal, and a small amount of mesquite sawdust to form barbecue briquettes for outdoor cooking. The sawdust in the briquettes imparts just enough mesquite flavor when burned to give that "western mesquite" flavor to meats smoked or grilled.

Considerable volumes of mesquite sawdust are also used in the liquid smoke industry. The sawdust is burned under controlled conditions, and the "smoke" is collected by condensing liquids in the smoke vapor on a cold surface. This mesquite-flavored liquid smoke is then further processed and either sold directly in the retail market or sold to large commercial meat processors for smoking various meat products. Much of the liquid smoke produced is also used as a flavor additive in other products such as potato chips, sauces, soups, and a multiplicity of powdered "secret" flavor mixes.

The mesquite barbecue industry often brings out Texans' entrepreneurial creativity in product development. The Mesquite Bean Cartel, a company in Abilene, Texas, has developed a new angle for supplying the mesquite's sweet smoke. It collects mesquite bean pods, dries them, and sells them in small and large bags throughout the United States to be used as barbecue flavoring. A handful of dry beans tossed on the coals will quickly impart mesquite's rich smoke aroma to meat.

A Mesquite Profile:
"A Funny Thing Happened on the Way to the Ski Slope!"
Jean and Rogers Craig, Marlin, Texas

Jean and Rogers Craig look at the rancher's nemesis, the mesquite, and think that nothing is more beautiful: everything is in the eye of the beholder. They've turned an obstacle on their ranch of 1,000 acres into a profitable business venture by selling mesquite cooking wood and firewood all over the world.

"It's something that we really look forward to," says Rogers Craig. "We get up every morning and look forward to our next adventure in the wood business." The main line of work of their company, named Brazos Valley Wood Products, is to take the gnarled, crooked mesquite tree into their manufacturing plant, chip it, chunk it, process it, dry it, package it, and ship it to customers. In business since the early 1980s, they both have seen the mesquite wood industry thrive and sputter. Back in the mid-1980s, with the oil crash in Texas, restaurants were dropping like flies, taking the wood business with them. Bankruptcies were commonplace. Craig says, "Out of over a hundred wood-processing companies that started business in the past seventeen years, only about four or five are still in operation."

The Craigs both laugh over how they first got into the wood business. Rogers retired from the Air Force in 1981; they were heading to Colorado to open a ski resort and stopped for a few weeks at the family ranch in Marlin. "We came to look around and enjoy the ranch for a couple of weeks," says Jean, "then head to Colorado for 'R an R' comprised of skiing, hiking, and golfing." A neighbor asked them if they could cut a few cords of wood for him and they said, "Sure, we sure can. After that, we got another order, then another." During a visit to the Texas Tumbleweed Restaurant in Dallas, the manager asked if they could supply him with ten cords of mesquite. "We looked at each other and said, 'Sure,' but really not knowing what ten cords of wood looked like. Now I know, a cord is 128 cubic feet," says Roger.

The mesquite craze was just beginning, and gourmet chefs in fancy restaurants from New York to California were calling to try to find mesquite. They all began emphasizing "mesquite grilled steaks and seafood." "At the time we delivered ten cords, the manager asked if we could supply seventeen cords a week to supply all of his seventeen restaurants. Now we are beginning to talk about work, and from that point on, we have never looked back, or regretted it, not one time." Brazos Valley Wood Products began with that first cord of wood and now is shipping hundreds of thousands of pounds of mesquite and hickory to the far reaches of the United States. Through supplying the Army/Air Force Exchange, they are sending mesquite around the world to military bases in Europe, Australia, and Japan and many other countries. Today, they are not only shipping barbecue wood, but are also heavily into the marketing of packaged firewood, which has really caught on. Convenience is the key to the cooking and firewood business. "You have to have the product in the form the customers want, when they want it and at the right price. It's the same with any sales business, satisfying the customers. That is probably why we survived the oil downturn in the mid-80s— we had good customers, treated them right, and we both benefited."

Their manufacturing plant includes a number of chop-saws, chunkers, hydraulic splitters, and a large number of pieces of support equipment. "At times it's like a military exercise, raw material coming in, the product going everywhere, wood cutters everywhere, equipment breaking down, truck drivers in and out, and everyone busy. Sometimes we think we can't do it, but somehow it all comes together and we get the job done." Jean is always toying with other product lines such as mesquite candy and gift packs for the Christmas season, as well as looking into the mesquite flooring business. They cut their wood from within forty miles of their ranch, buying some wood and at other times clearing land in exchange for the wood. They always have about thirty or so ranchers in waiting for clearing, with about another thirty expressing interest. Ranchers are not used to making money off their mesquite, only throwing money at it to have it eradicated.

"Ranchers despise mesquite," Rogers says. "I have ranchers just begging me to cut their mesquite. It's not an easy business, many ten-hour days, six or seven days a week depending on the season." They don't think about the time because it's their own business; personal enjoyment and the challenge of getting the job done motivate the couple, not the profit.

Not often do you hear of someone making something from nothing, but in the mesquite wood business that is just what entrepeneurs such as Jean and Rogers Craig are doing. "It's great to have a business where you get up and look forward to the day, and really get that satisfaction when you put all the parts together and get the job done. Helping the ranchers clear their rangelands and maybe making a few bucks off the pest of a tree is the sauce on top of the steak!"

Other companies have developed innovative products such as wax-coated, quick-light mesquite wood chunks and mesquite sawdust-based, extruded mini-logs. In the future many other innovative products will no doubt be developed and marketed in the mesquite barbecue industry.

How to Smoke and Barbecue with Mesquite
Contributed by Jean Craig, Marlin, Texas

Smoke cooking or barbecuing with mesquite is quite easy. Your success will depend on the type of cooker you are using, the size of the wood or the charcoal, the foods you are cooking, and the care you give to your barbecuing—the most important factor. First, pay attention to the type of cooker. There are as many outdoor cooking vessels as there are people who barbecue. Many are nice looking, and some are the most outlandish-looking things that you have ever seen, but most are very efficient. Some cookers are stationary "open pits" made of brick, stones, adobe, or whatever. Some have cooking areas that can be raised and lowered. Others have cooking surfaces that operate on a chain, with shelves that rotate from high in the cooker to down low to the fire. There are "kettle" cookers, hibachi cookers, and "barrel" cookers. Some kettle cookers look like flat hats with long skinny legs, while some are shaped like an upright hot dog, with two or three grill-rings that can be stacked one above the other, with short or long skinny legs. The hibachi cooker, generally made of thick aluminum or cast iron, is about twelve to fifteen inches long and about eight inches wide and is usually placed on a table. The barrel cooker is a long tube, such as a fifty-gallon drum or propane tank, from two to four feet in diameter; the lengths vary greatly, some barrel cookers being humongous. The larger ones are often on wheels and are moved around with a pickup truck. When looking for a barrel cooker, make sure it is made with new metal. If it is constructed from a used barrel or tank, it could previously have been used to hold pesticides or something else toxic—some of these "cides" cannot be washed from the metal. Some barrel cookers come with two sections: the larger end is used for smoke cooking and the smaller end, called the firebox, can be used for grilling. They have a smokestack that is usually at the end of the "smoke cooking" area, but sometimes at the other end. The smoke from the smokestack at the opposite end from the food that is cooking is the best for smoke cooking. Propane and electric cookers are also efficient ways to cook outdoors and have as many shapes and doodads as conventional wood-burning cookers. When looking for a cooker, be patient . . . find one that is right for you.

Mesquite for home use is available in three forms: two-inch chunks, chips (shavings or very small chips), and lump charcoal. Lump charcoal is irregular in shape because, unlike charcoal briquettes that are compressed by a machine, it is made the old-fashioned way, by burning solid mesquite wood. Lump charcoal is 100 percent wood, whereas briquettes often have clay fillers added and are also often made with coal "charcoal" rather than wood charcoal.

If you are using the two-inch mesquite chunks with lump charcoal or briquettes, soak them in warm water for up to twenty minutes (some people prefer beer and wine) and add them to the charcoal a few minutes before adding the food, allowing the wood to begin to smoke. Chips are handled in much the same way, but the smoking time is much reduced.

When using only mesquite chunks, begin the fire by stacking about fifteen to twenty mesquite chunks in a pyramid in the center of your cooking section or firebox. Soak them with fire starter or mineral spirits or use a fireblock wax starter and let the wood sit for a few minutes and then ignite the pyramid. Allow the fire to burn until a gray ash appears on the outside of the chunks and a lot of red glowing coals appear. If there are a few flames, wait a while longer for the fire to burn down or cover the cooker to suppress the fire or use the old spray bottle trick—squirt the fire out. The fire will be very hot, about 40 percent hotter than a briquette fire. Under the coal's surface, there will be some unburned wood—and that is where the great mesquite flavor is. The flavor of mesquite is rich, light, sweet, and woodsy, and it will not bite your tongue with a heavy taste. Because of the flavor and high heat produced by mesquite wood, it gives you a truly natural cooked taste.

When grilling steaks, pork chops, or anything with a fat rim, remove the fat, because the smoke produced by melting fat rises from the drips on the coals and interferes with the flavor being imparted by the mesquite. Vegetables are best quickly grilled, because if they are smoke-cooked the smoke will overcome their freshness. Just give the vegetables a light coating of olive oil, place them in a barbecue basket, and briskly grill them over the direct heat, allowing the mesquite to give them a little kiss of flavor.

Casseroles and corn in the husk may be cooked by indirect heat in a barbecue cooker. If you are using a Pyrex™ or stoneware bowl, wrap it with aluminum foil and, to keep the casserole from blackening, top it with a piece of aluminum foil that has dime-sized holes. This allows the smoke to weave in and out of the casserole, imparting mesquite's wonderful flavor. When you are cooking corn in the husk, pull the husk away from the corn but do not detach it. Remove all of the corn silk and dip the husk into a pail of warm water. Rewrap the husk around the corn, place it in the cooking area, and cook the corn for about thirty minutes.

The "greased paper grocery bag" method is the best method to use when smoke-cooking a turkey. Grease the bag inside and out, punching many small holes all over it. This allows the smoke to penetrate the bag, flavoring the turkey. When it is finished cooking, the turkey will have a pleasant pink color right under the skin. Should you forget the bag, the turkey will be completely black, but don't despair: remove the blackened skin and the turkey will be just as marvelous, with baby-pink meat. The mesquite flavor imparted to this magnificent bird is out of this world, so try it.

Seafood cooked over direct mesquite coals is wonderful. Shellfish and fish such as red snapper and flounder, cooked indirectly over mesquite, have a sumptuous taste.

Briskets are absolutely fantastic smoked with mesquite. Make sure your brisket has a good thick piece of fat on the top side. Take a fork and punch holes all over the fat, but not into the meat. Next, vigorously rub the seasoning into the fat and place the brisket into your cooker as far away from the fire as possible. Hold the temperature at around 200 to 250° F for about twenty hours and then remove the brisket from the cooker to an aluminum pan and cover tightly with aluminum foil. Return the pan to the cooker and allow the fire to die out slowly, over a period of two or three hours. Take out the brisket and place it on a cutting board, allowing it to rest at least thirty minutes. Remove the fat and soft gristle that run down through the center of the brisket and slice the brisket across the grain. When you serve your brisket, your guests will think they have died and gone to heaven. When cooking brisket "in the open," all that flavorful mesquite smoke will turn the meat black, but don't panic—that is the nature of mesquite smoke cooking.

Mesquite Jelly

Early settlers in the westward expansion days of the Southwest had to be very innovative in their selection of foods around the homestead. They had to rely on just what they grew from the soil and what could be collected from native plants. Traveling salespersons could only be expected once or twice each year, and their arrival was very unpredictable.

Sweet foods were hard to find in the 1800s on the western frontier. Sugar was a precious commodity purchased from traveling salespersons, and it was carefully rationed to last out the year. Jelly was one of the cherished sweets that tasted great with homemade flour biscuits made daily in the wood-fired ovens. Many wild fruits could be found, depending on the season—wild plums, wild peaches, crabapples, and mayhaws were plentiful during the spring and summer months. Through the years many homesteaders made jelly from the sweet mesquite pods, using various recipes. Mesquite jelly is delicious, having a light taste not unlike an apple or white grape jelly.

One jelly recipe, by Jean Craig of Marlin, Texas, has been passed down for years. Her recipe is easy to follow.

Mesquite Jelly

Ingredients:
2 pounds of whole mesquite beans to make 7 cups mesquite juice
2½ cups sugar
¼ cup sugar with 3 teaspoons pectin

Collect about two pounds of whole mesquite beans, place them into a pot, and add ten gallons of water. Simmer the beans for an hour until the water looks like dark clover honey. Pour out the liquid into a container. A lot of the flavor and sugar is still in the beans, so add a little water, sloshing it around the beans with a potato masher, boil to an iced-tea color, and add the liquid to the first stock. At this point you can freeze the stock in a plastic jug for later use.

To make the jelly, mix the ¼ cup of sugar and pectin well enough to distribute the pectin throughout the sugar. Bring the mesquite juice to a rolling boil, add the 2½ cups of sugar, and bring the juice mixture to a boil again. Add the sugar-pectin mixture and allow the juice to boil again for one minute. Pour it into sterilized jars and top them with sterilized lids. Turn the jars upside down until cool. Check the tops to make sure they are sealed. Now you have sweet, mild mesquite jelly.

All jellies will produce a foam as soon as the sugar is added to the boiling juice. In order to have clear jelly, this foam should be skimmed off as best you can.

The beans have to be picked at the correct time of the year, about the middle two weeks in September when the beans have completely dried on the tree. Use beans that are beige and beige with red stripes. The beans with the stripes are sweeter than the beige ones, but when they are mixed together you have a good flavor. Green pods are never used, as they impart a very bitter flavor to mesquite jelly.

Mesquite jelly turns to a coffee-brown color after about one year of storage, but it still has the great flavor of mesquite.

Mesquite jelly has been commercialized by two or three small cottage-sized manufacturers in Texas and marketed principally in the tourist shops and specialty food stores in major metropolitan cities.

Mesquite Pods as Human Food

As previously mentioned, people worldwide have used mesquite legume pods for food for thousands of years. The pods were usually converted into a flour that was further processed into cakes, biscuits, or nonalcoholic and alcoholic beverages. Various means of preparation were used, but the vast majority of methods essentially ground the pods into flour or into a meal. Today, in many "Third World" locations of the world, tree legumes such as mesquites are the only consistent, predictable source of flour during times of extreme drought and pestilence and are the only food stock that lies between survival and starvation.

Mesquite pods naturally are rich in sugars, proteins, fat, and fiber. People throughout the years have recognized the food merits of mesquite pods. J. Frank Dobie, in his 1941 *Arizona Highways* article, wrote: "In the days of the Texas Republic, or shortly thereafter, Elisha A. Briggs, a Texas ranger, found some Mexican freighters who had been raided by Indians, living on prickly pear apples, mesquite beans, and rattlesnakes. He asked an old Mexican how long a person could live on such a diet. The Mexican answered: 'Con tuna solo se puede vivir, pero con tunas y mesquites los dos se engorda mucho.' ('With pear apples alone one can live, but with pear apples and mesquite beans also a person will get big fat.')."

Mesquite pods are composed of two parts, the pericarp (the outer covering, sweet pulp, and the hard seed husk) and the seed. The hard seed husk contains most of the sugar and fiber, and the seed contains most of the protein and fat. The sugar content of mesquite pods in the form of sucrose is high, ranging from 13 to 34 percent. Proteins in mesquite pods are primarily located in the seed, which contains about 39 percent proteins, much higher than traditional commercial legumes such as green peas, which are about 20 to 22 percent protein. When the pods are dried to about 5 percent moisture content, they are easily milled to a flour in either a hammermill or a stonemill.

In spite of the high nutrient content of mesquite pods, the potential commercialization of a mesquite pod flour enterprise is not promising in regions where there are available grain flours. Mesquite pod flour has a distinctively abnormal flavor, a very coarse texture, and a reduced baking quality. Tests of cakes and breads using high proportions of mesquite flour showed that it was not an acceptable replacement for traditional grain flours, although preparations using half mesquite and half wheat flour could be acceptable for certain breads and cookies. The most promising area for the commercialization of mesquite pod processing, marketing, and human consumption is in regions of the world with high poverty and the absence of alternative grain flours. Plantations of mesquite trees in extremely arid and poverty-stricken locations such as parts of Brazil and India are directed toward this purpose. In these areas mesquite pods may be the only available food stock for the preparation of various bread products.

The Mesquite in Verse

Mesquite has had a place in the poetry of southwestern poets for more than 150 years. One could surmise that, for centuries, the Indians had their own forms of poetry expressing their reverence for the mesquite and honoring it for supplying many of their daily needs. Three poets of the twentieth century have placed mesquite in verse in such a way that we can truly imagine what the tree symbolized to the early Southwest travelers and homesteaders.

Frank Grimes

Throughout the southwestern United States, there is a story told of spring not arriving until the mesquites bud out. It is said that peaches, pecan, and other fruit and many other wild plants and trees will bud out too early in the spring and get killed-back by late freezes, but never the mesquite.

Frank Grimes, former *Abilene Reporter-News* editor for more than forty years and renowned newspaper poet, wrote a famous poem in 1928 that has become a part of the west Texas folklore that brought notoriety to this "fact."

The Old Mesquites Ain't Out

We see some signs of returning spring—
The redbird's back and the fie' larks sing.
The ground's plowed up and the creeks run clear,
The onions sprout and the rosebud's near;
And yet they's a point worth thinkin' about—
We note
that the old
mesquites
ain't out!

The fancier trees are in full bloom,
The grass is green and the willows boom,
The colts kick up and the calves bend down,
And the spring's a-pear-ently come to town;
And yet they's a point worth thinkin' about—
        We note
                that the old
                        mesquites
                                ain't out!

Well, it may be spring for all we know—
There ain't no ice and there ain't no snow,
It looks like spring and it smells so too,
The cal-en-dar says it's plenty true—
And yet they's a point worth thinkin' about—
        We note
                that the old
                        mesquites
                                ain't out!

Old-timers will swear not only that this is true, but that the mesquite has even outpredicted the weather forecasters relying on the most exotic instrumentation. Most west Texans consider that the danger of a late frost no longer exists if mesquite leaves have begun to emerge. Unseasonably warm weather in Texas in February and early March usually results in bud burst in ornamental and other shrubs and trees, but seldom in the mesquite.

Mesquite does appear to have this ability of predicting just the correct time for bud break. Scientists have said that apparently some plants, like the mesquite, can tolerate a lengthy cold period of below-freezing temperatures; if that cold period does not occur or is less severe, bud break is delayed. This is the case with the mesquite. The more consecutive cold days occurring in January and February, the earlier bud break occurs. Once the winter chilling requirements are met, warm temperatures after mid-February hasten the date of bud break.

Mesquite's great dimensional stability makes it an ideal medium for fine wood turnings such as this vessel crafted by Jim Lee of Reagan Wells, Texas. (Photo © Jim Lee, master wood turner, Reagan Wells, Texas)

Faye Carr Adams

Born in Lavor, Texas, Faye Carr Adams grew up talking to the cowboys at the Prude Ranch about ranch life and early times in Texas. These early experiences enabled her to write poems about her amazement at the mesquite's toughness and its ability to withstand all the adversities that nature could deal it. Adams, a member of the Poetry Society of Texas and the Poetry Society of London, wrote many poems illustrating the hard life of the early Southwest settlers and ranchers. Many of her poems were published in two collections, *More Than a Loaf* and *Sweet Is the Homing Hour.*

Adams's poetry expressed these early Texans' thoughts and feelings about the mesquite, which evolved over two centuries. In "Where Longhorn Bones Lie Bleached," Adams extols mesquite's superior strength to withstand the most extreme conditions. Mesquite's ability not to be fooled by the "northers" that blow through Texas in the early spring, killing-back most of the other shrubs and trees, is the essence of her poem "Mesquite."

It took poets such as Faye Carr Adams to put mesquite's true nature and character in verse.

Where Longhorn Bones Lie Bleached

(from *More Than a Loaf*, 46–47)

Mesquite will grow,
Defiant and alone,
Where land is suckled dry
And set with stone.
Where longhorn bones lie bleached
Too dry to rot,
Mesquite, tough as steer hide,
Offers golden bloom for bees,
Shade for mourning doves;
And sweet bean pods
To gaunt and staggering maverick

Or raw-boned man.
Mesquite thorns sharpened on transient rain
While every cruising wind piledrives its roots.
But man curses it—
Dulls his axe against its crippled trunk,
Pulls it from the lonely land,
Then sets the fire to burn its heart at stake.
Even on the last altar,
Mesquite has strength;
Its pungent smoke rallies
To season the Texas sky.

Mesquite

(from *Sweet Is the Homing Hour*, 52)

Mesquite
Is strangely wise
To Winter's fickle way
Of sudden northers on a late
Spring day.

Mesquite
withholds her growth,
Wary, while foolish trees
Flaunt new green buds to die in a
Late freeze.

Boyce House

Born in Piggot, Arkansas, Boyce House had a career as an author, humorist, and radio personality that took him to many locations in Texas. Working in eleven different communities, including newspaper jobs in Eastland, Ranger, Cisco, Olney, and Fort Worth, he wrote many humorous columns and books about Texas. His weekly column appeared in 130 newspapers. A weekly radio program brought him celebrity status in Texas and gave him a prominent reputation nationwide.

In these travels that took him throughout much of mesquite country for over half a century, House developed an uncanny feel for the mesquite tree and its place in defining the character of Texas and an understanding of the tenacity of the southwestern landscape. His writing, particularly his poem "The Mesquite," reveals the thoughts and feelings of many early Texans, portraying mesquite as 'A very parody of a Tree—." House depicts the extremely adverse conditions in which the mesquite not only survives but thrives, making it the noblest of trees.

The Mesquite

Many poems have been written about trees—
Oaks, willows, elms and pines;
Poplars, palms, cedars and hemlocks:
Trees that are slender,
Others wide-spreading and strong,
That are a song to the eye, a feast to the ear—
Deep shade and tuneful branches, wind-swept and bird
haunted.

But no poet has ever sung of one tree—
an outcast, an Ishmael,
The mesquite,
it grows in the West:
Its wood is so tough it dulls the keenest axe-blade:
Its fruit—the gaudy mesquite-bean—is little more than an
apple of Sodom:
Its shade is thin and ragged:
And its form is weird and twisted.
A very parody of a tree—
Yes, the gods were laughing (you say) when they made the
mesquite—
The clown in the parade of growing things.
But your proud trees are in lands of rains, streams, and
rich loams:
The mesquite dares to grow in a region where the air is
crinkled with the heat,

The hills pant,
And the lizards lie breathless under the shade of rocks that
 are wrinkled and colorless;
The sand stretches as glaring and parched as a beach whose
 ocean has died.
Only the thorny cactus grows there—and the brave mesquite.
Its frailly-fringed boughs flaunt like green flags in the
 face of advancing foes.
Horse and rider rest under its branches at noon
After a little fire has been built of old mesquite limbs—
The aroma of the coffee and of the wood-smoke is very
 sweet—
(There is no other quite like it in the world).

And at night the moon is kind to the mesquite:
The gnarled outline is softened and silvered,
And the tree dreams of sighing waters, and lyrical birds,
 and laughing lovers.

Worldwide Aspects of Prosopis

Prosopis is quickly becoming one of the most important tree species for multiple uses in many regions of the world. Drylands worldwide now comprise about one-third of the land base and are on an upward growth trend. Many, if not most, of these dryland sites have severe shortages of many essential natural resources vital to a healthy society's development. Resources such as fuelwood, trees for shade, forage for livestock and wildlife, soil-stabilizing and enriching trees, and both human foods and livestock fodder are dangerously absent in many of these drylands. Without these resources, individuals, communities, and society as a whole stay stagnant, struggling for existence and survival with few growth prospects.

Although it has provided benefits to dryland sites worldwide, *Prosopis* has escaped control in several locations, such as Australia and Sudan, where it was introduced as a beneficial tree and has become a tremendous pest encroaching on valuable fertile farmlands. *Prosopis* is a very aggressive tree and must be cautiously kept under close management. In several cases, farmland infestation by *Prosopis* has become a larger problem than the conditions that existed in the arid lands before its introduction.

Prosopis, whether native or introduced, has many favorable attributes and characteristics under proper management and is becoming a major player in the development of solutions to these societal development constraints. Its role is sure to expand as we go into the next millennium.

Use of Prosopis *in Combating Worldwide Desertification*

Prosopis is intensively used worldwide in combating the desertification of arid lands. Desertification essentially is the destruction of the biological potential of land in dry areas under the combined pressures of adverse and fluctuating climate and excessive exploitation. Most areas of desertification are in two geographical belts, approximately centered on the Tropics of Cancer and Capricorn, 23.5 degrees north and south of the equator. Desertified areas are not strictly deserts, but can be on the fringes of natural deserts.

As mentioned, drylands cover more than a third of the earth's land surface. More than 80 percent of these lands are found in the continents of Africa (37 percent), Asia (33 percent), and Australia (14 percent). The most arid lands, termed "hyper-arid" and "arid," receive less than one inch and ten inches of rain per year, respectively.

Five Major Desertification Zones Worldwide

1. The Afro-Asian belt from the Atlantic Ocean to China.
2. The North American Desert of the southwestern United States and northwestern Mexico.
3. The Atacama Desert between the Andes and the Pacific Ocean from Ecuador to central Chile and the Patagonian Desert of Argentina.
4. The Namib and Kalahari Deserts of southern Africa.
5. The Australian Desert.

Prosopis is playing a role in the effort to convert hyper-arid and arid lands to more productive and stable grazing land. One of the main characteristics of desertification is the degradation of soil and vegetation. Deforestation makes soil more susceptible to wind and water erosion, and desertification is accelerated by declines in soil fertility and structure. Vegetation is considered degraded when the land can no longer support what it could be expected to support given the site and climate or provide what is needed for environmental protection.

Drought is one major factor in desertification, as it exacerbates poor land use practices such as overcultivation, overgrazing, deforestation, and mismanagement of irrigation, cropland, and water resources. With overgrazing, valuable perennial grasses and browse shrubs do not have time to regenerate, eventually disappearing. Without natural regeneration, improvement in the site will require seeding or planting of desirable fodder plants.

Prosopis is one of the most valuable fodder plants and has been extensively introduced in locations such as India. *Prosopis* is a "multipurpose" tree cropped for fodder and fuelwood and made into many products such as housing, flooring, and fencing. The tree is highly drought resistant and saline tolerant, and it bears pods containing up to 14 percent protein and 44–55 percent carbohydrate. *Prosopis* can grow in areas receiving less than four inches of rainfall annually, burrowing its taproot deep into the soil to tap into the water table. There is some evidence that *Prosopis* can take up water from the atmosphere through its leaves if water is not available in the soil. Because of its extreme saline tolerance, *Prosopis* will grow in soils with a pH of 9.5 to 10.0 and a soluble salt content of 0.54 to 1.0 percent. Worldwide, it is being planted on extremely saline sites, making these lands productive again.

Much research is still needed to find suitable species and refine cultural practices in order for *Prosopis* and other species of multipurpose trees to attain their full potential in combating desertification. The International Board for Plant Genetic Resources (IBPGR) identified *Prosopis* as one of four multipurpose tree genera for use in arid and semiarid lands. Through this effort, several species of *Prosopis* from South America (*Prosopis alba*, *Prosopis chilensis*, *Prosopis juliflora*, *Prosopis nigra*, *Prosopis pallida*, and *Prosopis tamarugo*) have been identified as meeting the criteria and have been introduced and naturalized in many parts of Asia, Africa, and Australia. Research and many reforestation plantings of *Prosopis* are ongoing throughout the world.

Algarrobo in South America

Algarrobo, as mesquite is called in most South American countries, has been an essential plant for animals and humans for thousands of years. Its bean pods have been used for both animal and human feedstock since the earliest human records. At a site near Punammurea, Argentina, at an elevation of around 11,500 feet, evidence was found of algarrobo pods associated with human remains in mountain caves. The pods were determined to be *Prosopis nigra*, and subsequent carbon dating of the pods and seeds gave a date of about 8600 B.C. It is astonishing to think that some six thousand years before the pyramids were built an ancient Argentinian taking refuge in a mountain cave was eating algarrobo beans.

The word "algarrobo" normally refers to the carob tree (*Ceratonia siliqua*) from the Mediterranean region. When Spanish explorers first came upon the southwestern Indians using mesquite, they named it algarrobo because of its similarity to the carob tree in form and use as a legume. South America, particularly Argentina, is thought to be the area of origin of the *Prosopis* genus, and it is a center of diversity of algarrobo, where most of its varying characteristics and species are represented. It is hypothesized that millions of years ago mammals and large birds dispersed algarrobo seeds over the long distances to North America and other regions of the world. Researchers believe that over the thousands of years after the initial dispersal another center of diversity of species with unique characteristics developed in the Mexican-Texan region.

When the Spanish conquistadors traveled through northern Argentina and Chile in the sixteenth and seventeenth centuries, they encountered Indians using a twisted, gnarled tree with edible fruit. Algarrobas (the fruit or pod of the algarrobo tree) provided a means of survival during times when starvation was imminent and no other food plants were present. Like the Indians in the southwestern region of North America, the early South American Indians were dependent on the algarrobo for foods, medicines, structural timbers, fuel, and many other crucial daily-life items. The Atacama Indians of Chile ate corn for six months of the year and depended on algarrobo for the other six months. The fruits of the algarrobo provided bean pod flour that was ground and made into a type of bread called *patay* and a fermented alcoholic wine called *chica*.

Today algarrobo wood is used extensively for home cooking fuel and timber. Many local residents in algarrobo country harvest small stems, dry them, and use them for heating and cooking in their homes. Algarrobo timbers are employed in the construction of dwellings, wagons, and barrels and are used in the home for furniture, flooring, and other utilitarian and decorative purposes.

In Camalan, in the arid northeastern Brazilian state of Paraíba, a manufacturing facility to process algarroba pods as animal fodder has been in operation since 1988. This facility supplies thousands of tons of pods to commercial poultry and pig-raising enterprises, enabling them to stay in business during times of drought. The northeastern region of Brazil comprises more than 450,000 acres of arid, shallow soil lands with low annual rainfall; the rural dwellers of the region live in poverty and are dependent on the land for subsistence. Vast acreage of algarrobo is being planted and managed for the purpose of pod harvest after five or six years for processing into flour, which is eventually converted into cakes and biscuits for human consumption.

As in San Antonio, Texas, algarrobo was widely used in past years in paving most of the streets and major avenues of Buenos Aires and many other large cities in Argentina. During extensive street repairs, street beds of algarrobo placed in sand beds a hundred or more years ago can often still be found today. Layer after layer of asphalt road surfaces have been laid on top, and the blocks are still functioning well.

Mirroring the problems with honey mesquite in Texas, venal or chamacoco (*Prosopis ruscifolia*) has become a relentless, aggressive agricultural pest, infesting thousands of acres of rangelands in Argentina, Bolivia, Paraguay, and Brazil. The reasons for this infestation are basically the same as in Texas: the overgrazing of livestock, the suppression of plant-killing wildfires, and the extreme drought cycles that took place in the 1930s. All these factors contributed greatly to the infestation problem. Unlike honey mesquite and velvet mesquite in Texas, algarrobo in many parts of South America has greatly extended its range and increased its stand density on new sites. It has taken over millions of historically fertile grasslands in Argentina in the state of Formosa and in the Chaco region. As in the United States, massive mechanical and herbicide treatments for eradication and control are ongoing, utilizing large crawler tractors and aerial spraying of herbicides.

In contrast, human-planted tamarugo (*Prosopis tamarugo*) plantations are being established in the Tamarugal Pampa area of Chile and are transforming the desert into an agro-ecosystem. Agricultural productivity has increased greatly in this area of South America—one of the most inhospitable regions on the face of the earth. In a practice called "silvopasture," projects in Peru and Chile plant trees such as *Prosopis* on rangelands to increase the productivity of livestock. Integrating *Prosopis* stands with grazing lands on Peru's Pacific coast and in

Chile allows for the harvest of *Prosopis* fodder and pods for fattening pigs and cattle in feedlots. Plantations of *Prosopis* were planted on barren wastelands created by deforestation in the past and are now producing from ten to fourteen tons of pods per acre. Tamarugo can survive and even thrive in soils with high salinity and low fertility. The species, which usually needs nine inches of rainfall annually, has adapted to areas receiving as little as three inches or less. Tamarugo, which grows year-round to heights of thirty-six feet, can withstand long periods of drought while still producing abundant seed pods for both livestock and human consumption.

Today algarrobo wood is being utilized commercially in a small cottage industry in Argentina and other countries in South America for various products such as flooring and furniture for local homes and businesses and for artistic sculptures and turnings for the tourist trade. The transfer of techniques and technology between Argentina and Texas has assisted both regions in developing further markets and new products for the algarrobo industry.

Mesquite in Mexico

Mesquite is found in the northern and central states of Mexico and throughout the Baja Peninsula. Nine *Prosopis* species grow there. The most common species, *Prosopis glandulosa*, has aggressively invaded thousands of acres of rangeland in northern Mexico.

In contrast to the situation in the United States, mesquite is used widely in Mexico for many products such as firewood, sawlogs, fencing posts and boards, barks for tanning, and solid wood products such as furniture, flooring, and crafts to sell to the tourist trade. The use of mesquite in the daily lives of many Mexicans is so intense that it has led to excessive harvest of mesquite stands, generating the need to reforest much of the land with mesquite. Reforestation will stabilize the growth/harvest balance of mesquite, lead to an improvement in the quality of life for rural residents, and help diversify the local economic activities. Without reforestation, the sustained availability of mesquite for present and future demands is in question.

Archaeological records of mesquite's use in Mexico as human food date back to the Chichimecan Indian hunters and gatherers who wandered throughout the highlands of San Luis Potosí gathering mesquite pods, which were eaten as fresh fruit or conserved in a solution of their own sweet juice. Bean pod flour was made for breadlike food and also mixed with water and allowed to ferment into an alcoholic beverage. Remains of mesquite pods in caves in the Tehuacán Valley indicate that mesquite pods were eaten by people as early as 6500 B.C. Today mesquite bark, gum, and foliage are used by some local people in rural areas to combat gastritis, as an antiseptic, and as an anti-dysenteric.

Table 12. Species of Mesquite in Mexico

NUMBER OF SPECIES	SPECIES
9	*P. reptans* var. *cinerascens*, *P. pubescens*, *P. palmeri*, *P. articulata*, *P. tamaulipana*, *P. laevigata*, *P. juliflora*, *P. glandulosa* var. *glandulosa*, var. *prostrata*, var. *torreyana* *P. velutina*

Source: Burkart 1976.

The first cannon used in Mexico's fight for independence from Spain was hollowed out of mesquite. In need of artillery, the Mexicans split a mesquite log, hollowed it out, then bound the halves with green cowhide. The 1810 cannon worked well and is now on exhibit at the National Museum in Mexico City.

Over the past century, mesquite bean pods have been used as vital forage, enabling livestock to survive significant long-term droughts. Today some rural populations still collect dry pods for their animals and store them for use during drought periods. In the state of San Luis

Potosí in 1982, one rural cooperative collected more than 3,000 tons of pods used to manufacture concentrated livestock feed.

Charcoal is one of Mexico's major products manufactured from mesquite. Many small mesquite enterprises make charcoal by the process of incomplete combustion from wood placed in large pits. The wood is placed in the pit, covered by soil, and ignited. The wood burns slowly with limited oxygen, leaving wood charcoal in the pit. Mexico's average annual mesquite charcoal production over the past twenty-five years is more than 2,770 tons, the majority of which (estimated at 70 percent) is exported to the United States. Most of the domestic charcoal production in the United States has been replaced by charcoal from Mexico, where the producers have the advantage of low costs for labor, transportation, and wood. In the past, entire communities in Mexico depended on mesquite charcoal for their livelihood, but forest management controls by governmental forestry authorities and the lack of large logs have limited charcoal production in many communities.

Mesquite furniture and flooring production has increased greatly over the past twenty-five years in the Mexican states of Zacatecas and Guanajuato. In Guanajuato particularly, sawing and milling of mesquite logs into furniture has become one of the most important industries in the state.

Small shops that work mesquite are widespread in Mexico's mesquite country, generating the greater part of many woodworkers' incomes. These shops make wood turnings, sculptures, and animal figurines sold in tourist and handicraft shops throughout the region and exported to the United States.

Prosopis *in Asia and Africa*

Prosopis grows extensively in the northernmost Indian regions of Punjab, West Rajasthan, Gujarat, and Uttar Pradesh and in the drier parts of central and southern India, and also in Pakistan, Afghanistan, Iran, and Arabia. Six species are present in Asia: *Prosopis cineraria*, *Prosopis farcta* vars. *farcta* and *glabra*, and *Prosopis koelziana* are native; *Prosopis glandulosa*, *Prosopis juliflora*, and *Prosopis pallida* were introduced in programs to combat desertification. *Prosopis cineraria*, also referred to as

Prosopis spicigera, is by far the major species in land coverage and in utilization. It is used extensively for many day-to-day purposes, such as for firewood, for animal fodder, and in the production of timber.

The common name for mesquite, and for *Prosopis cineraria* specifically, varies from region to region—it is called jand and khejri in India, ghaf in Arabia, and jand in Pakistan, khejri being the most widespread name. Khejri is a very thorny tree, reaching a height of about forty feet with a widespread, open crown. It grows on sites with varying characteristics, from alluvial and coarse sandy soils to extremely alkaline and saline locations. Khejri has been reported to grow in soil with a pH of more than 9.8.

Because of its heaviness and fast growth, khejri is preferred over almost all tree species in India for the production of stovewood for cooking and home heating. Exceptionally fine charcoal is manufactured from khejri in India, and it is used extensively for animal fodder not only because its leaves are very palatable and nutritious, but also because farmers can rely on it being present in times of drought. Local farmers in many areas consider it the best browse tree to plant for livestock such as sheep, cattle, and camels. Both the foliage and pods of the *Prosopis* can be used as fodder. In India *Prosopis juliflora* and *Prosopis cineraria* trees are "lopped" for fodder every winter without harming future growth. Throughout the year its leaves and pods are browsed by sheep and cattle.

Where many other tree species have succumbed, khejri, which can withstand extreme drought, has been planted extensively to combat the advance of the Thar desert toward New Delhi. Thousands of trees have been planted in belts miles long in an attempt to slow this process. Research is ongoing in Pakistan and India, investigating various planting methods, seed germination, seedling culture, and tree care to combat this growing menace.

Windbreaks, which protect soils, crops, and livestock on farmlands worldwide from hot, desiccating winds, are being created using *Prosopis* trees. *Prosopis* was one of the trees in a three-zone windbreak system used on more than 2,400 miles of roadside windbreaks in the state of Rajasthan, India. In Nigan's Majjia Valley, 523 miles of *Prosopis*, acacia, and eucalyptus windbreaks were constructed in an area near Booiga for protection of valuable topsoil on which villages grow sorghum and millet.

Due to its ability to increase the fertility of soils by facilitating the fixing of atmospheric nitrogen and contributing beneficial organic matter, khejri is being planted in India between annual row crops by many farmers. Khejri is not considered a significant competitor for available soil moisture because rowcrops draw their moisture from the topsoil while its taproot reaches deep into the soil. On these intensively farmed sites, farmers consider that the benefits of khejri outweigh its use of some soil moisture. Khejri provides shade to crops during the extremely hot summer months by slowing evapo-transpiration. Wheat, maize, sorghum, and pearl millet are some of the crops grown with khejri on Indian farms.

Prosopis has also played a vital role in the Sahel, a fringe area of the Sahara Desert extending across north-central Africa from latitude ten degrees south to latitude sixteen degrees north and from the Atlantic to the Indian Oceans. Severe droughts have ravaged these lands for years, causing the destruction of millions of trees and producing a shortage of energy and food and a reduction of soil fertility. Rainfall has been limited to less than 25 inches annually, mostly from June to October. A recent priority in tree management has been the development of multipurpose, fast-growing, nitrogen-fixing leguminous trees such as *Prosopis*.

Prosopis has been used in extensive "town greenbelts" in and around Nouakchott, capital of Mauritania. Being about 70 percent Sahara Desert, for years this area has been threatened by tremendous sandstorms and encroaching sand dunes. The most significant cause of these encroaching arid lands is that an area several miles wide was stripped of all trees and shrubs by nomads fleeing the drought-stricken interior, who used the wood for housing and cooking fuelwood. In 1975 the planting of 283 acres of drought-resistant *Prosopis chilensis* began an extensive effort to combat this problem, providing a windbreak for the city. These managed trees will eventually be utilized to help supply the huge demand for fuelwood and other uses for city dwellers.

Prosopis trees are being used as "living fences" at Darda in Chad, replacing the traditional fences made from dead thorn tree branches. After a protection period of four to five years, the trees will be large enough to be used as fodder and as a source of pods and for products such as poles and fuelwood.

Prosopis africana is the only *Prosopis* species that is native to Senegal, one of the many countries of the Sahel. *Prosopis africana* has been overexploited as firewood and timber, resulting in severe shortages. Its leaves and pods are used as forage and in traditional medicines. *Prosopis juliflora*, as well as *Prosopis alba* and *Prosopis cineraria*, was introduced from Central America in the early 1800s and is now the most important and most common *Prosopis* species in the area. Since its introduction, it has provided pods and leaves for forage during times of long-term drought when other plants are not available and is also utilized in windbreaks to stabilize the sandy soil of the region.

As previously mentioned, introduction of drought-resistant *Prosopis* trees to halt the spread of deserts can have a very negative impact if not kept under close management and can eventually become as great a concern as the encroaching desert. For example, in the Sudan *Prosopis*, which was introduced by the British in 1937 for the purpose of improving the desert, has escaped management controls. Spread by cattle and birds, it has invaded hundreds of thousands of acres of rich farmlands in eastern and central Sudan.

In the 1970s and 1980s, during a time when Sudan was experiencing cyclic droughts that caused the desert to advance about ten miles per year, *Prosopis* was thought to be the savior tree and was planted widely across the country, where it subsequently escaped controls. Recent studies have concluded that the escaped *Prosopis* is spreading at a rate of one thousand acres per year, causing difficulty in farming Sudan's fertile lands and drying up scarce underground water resources. The effect of *Prosopis* on Sudan's farmlands has been so significant that the government has passed a law to eradicate *Prosopis* from the country. Sudan's minister of agriculture has stated that "the effect of mesquite on the environment and natural resources is more dangerous than that of the drought" (The Miracle Trees That Drank the Water, 1997). Sudan has initiated tree eradication campaigns throughout the country.

The effect of *Prosopis* on Sudan's farmlands and the plans for its eradication are not without controversy. The Sudanese Environment Conservation Society has described the government's war on *Prosopis* as an overreaction and recommended that the trees should be controlled instead of being eradicated. Although studies have shown that

Prosopis consumes a great deal of underground water, the same studies show that the tree's roots make the soil porous enough for the rain water to seep into the ground. Without the *Prosopis* roots, rain water will not infiltrate into the clay soil and will be lost through evaporation. The tree escaped control because of poor farm management; but, under management and control, it reduces wind velocity, protects crops from sand dunes, provides animal fodder, and supplies fuel and building materials. No ready replacement exists for *Prosopis* in the deforested areas of Sudan if it is eradicated.

The Australian Experience

Prosopis species are not native to the Australian continent, but at least six species have been introduced: *Prosopis flexuosa*, *Prosopis pallida*, *Prosopis chilensis*, *Prosopis juliflora*, *Prosopis glandulosa*, and *Prosopis velutina*. They have become naturalized in the states of New South Wales, South Australia, Queensland, and Western Queensland. All of the *Prosopis* species in Australia, called spiny prosopis or just mesquite, are believed to be of North or South American origin. Two of the species, *Prosopis flexuosa* and *Prosopis pallida*, are classified by the Queensland Lands Department as range pest plants in inland Queensland and further south through the state of South Australia, although when they were introduced they were not considered pests.

Across Australia there has always been a severe shortage of livestock fodder and shade during times of extreme drought, and native grasses and other forage plants cannot supply an adequate amount of fodder for livestock survival. Drought-hardy fodder trees such as *Prosopis* are deep rooted and supply shade, leaves, and protein- and sugar-rich beans for livestock survival. During times of drought most range grasses burn off, leaving these short shrubs and trees as the only food source.

Around 1900 *Prosopis* was introduced on thousands of acres in Queensland to meet the need for a drought-hardy fodder source. Due to its aggressive growth, *Prosopis*, especially *Prosopis glandulosa* and *Prosopis juliflora*, escaped management control, invading much of the grasslands and creek banks. Combined with the replacement of sheep by cattle, which masticate mesquite seed much more than sheep and disperse the seed much more effectively and extensively, this has caused a tremendous brush problem not unlike the large-scale infestations of mesquite in the southwestern United States, due to many of the same factors. The causes in Australia include overgrazing by domestic livestock; overgrazing by feral animals such as horses, donkeys, goats, pigs, camels, and rabbits; and excessive usage of artesian waters by humans. Dense thickets of mesquite have developed in Australia, where it successfully competes with native trees and forage grasses for both nutrients and scarce soil moisture. Management measures in Australia mirror those of the programs in the southwestern United States.

One program recently initiated to assist in combating the encroaching mesquite is the introduction of biological control agents. Two mesquite seed–feeding bruchid beetles, *Algarobius prosopis* and *Algarobius battimeri,* have been introduced on mesquite rangelands to assist in controlling its spread.

Texas Ebony—Mesquite's Astonishing Cousin

Growing in south Texas near the Rio Grande and in the northern states of Mexico along with honey mesquite is a tree that produces one of the hardest, heaviest, and blackest woods known to humankind: Texas ebony. If you attempt to hammer a nail into it, your hammer will kick back with a tremendous force—it is almost impossible to drive in the nail. This wood weighs about 65.5 pounds per cubic foot, making it heavier than water's 62.4 pounds per cubic foot: when a chunk is placed in a pail of water, it sinks quickly to the bottom like a lead weight.

Texas ebony (or "apes-earrings" or "ebony blackbeard" as it is often called, because of its black, beaded or segmented pods) grows in areas similar to sites where the crooked, short-stemmed mesquite is found. It reaches a height of about thirty to forty feet and a diameter of up to two and one-half feet. As with the mesquite, long and wide unblemished lumber is hard to find, but the wood is exquisite. Texas ebony wood has a dark, blackish, swirling grain and upon fine sanding finishes to a fantastic sheen. It is as hard as nails, causing much dulling of saw blades, planer blades, and bandsaw blades.

Texas ebony's common name is inaccurate; it is called an ebony due to its black, hard, and heavy wood, but it is not an ebony according to scientific classification. True ebonies are trees of the genus *Diospyros*, represented by the common persimmon (*Diospyros virginiana*) in the United States and the Texas persimmon or Mexican persimmon (*Diospyros texana*) in Texas and south of the border. Texas ebony, whose scientific name, *Pithecellobium flexicaule*, refers to its sweet bean pulp and its very flexuous branches, is a very close relative of the mesquite. Its legume pod, unlike mesquite's flat pod, has a rounded profile, being 4 to 6 inches long, very dark brown to black, and segmented in appearance. Its leaves are also pinnately compound, about 1 to 2 inches long, composed of one to three pairs of pinnae, with the lowest pair normally shorter. It has three to five leaflets per pinna, each about ⅕ to ½ inch long. Its flowers are yellow spikes about 1 to 1½ inches long; they bloom in the spring and continue through much of the summer.

Texas ebony wood in Mexico, where the tree is called ébano, is used primarily for posts, fuel, furniture, and cabinetry. It is a very showy ornamental tree with exceptionally beautiful and predictable blooms. Because of its attractiveness, it is often planted as a shade tree in yards, public gardens, and along roadsides in south Texas and is widely considered the most valuable shade tree in the lower Rio Grande Valley region of Texas. The seeds are collected and eaten by many Mexican families, after being prepared by either boiling when green or roasting when ripe.

In the United States Texas ebony wood is largely used as an accent for other distinctive woods of contrasting colors and sheen, especially mesquite. Mesquite's rich, dark, reddish-brown color is complemented by inlays of Texas ebony's black wood in many exquisite works of art such as desks and tables, rocking chairs, and jewelry boxes. Ebony wood is used by itself for wood turnings and sculptures; the marvelous sheen of this rich, black, grainy wood has great beauty.

The bean family includes many trees with unique characteristics and beauty. The Texas ebony matches its cousin the mesquite in rivaling the exotic tropical hardwoods of the world. Word of Texas ebony wood's classic beauty, its great working properties, and its availability has generated a growing interest in its use.

Mesquite wood is superior for application where high dimensional stability and extreme hardness are indispensable, as in the varsity weight rooms at the Department of Athletics at Texas A&M University in College Station. (Photo © Ken E. Rogers)

Mesquite's Future

Mesquite's significance to humankind in the twenty-first century will become much greater than its current limited importance, possibly approaching the major role it had over the past centuries in the lives of the Southwest Indians. In this age of increasing world populations, diminishing resources and emphasis on renewable resources, and an increased ecological responsibility and awareness, more intensive management of the mesquite ecosystem and even of individual mesquite trees that thrive on marginal lands will come to the forefront. Mesquite's ability to grow on marginally unusable arid lands and provide wood products, livestock fodder, nitrogen and organic matter for the soil, and a feedstock for energy and chemical processes and products will stimulate increased interest in this unique genus, *Prosopis*.

Future Areas of New and Increased Mesquite Utilization

- Fine veneers for plywood for use in furniture, paneling, etc.
- Increased ornamental usage for arid landscape plantings
- Feedstock for chemicals and pharmaceuticals
- Wood extractives conversion into wood plastics
- Greater usage in worldwide desertification projects
- Growing for biomass farms for energy feedstock
- Increased harvest of mesquite pods for human and livestock consumption
- Increased use in packaged firewood
- Increased use in flooring and the development of efficient production systems
- Growing of plantations of straight-stemmed mesquite for lumber production

Research activities emphasizing mesquite ecosystem and individual mesquite tree management will increase. Due to its ability to withstand drought, mesquite will be used much more in desertification efforts in arid areas. As improved trees are selected for desirable growth characteristics and drought hardiness, mesquite application will become more widespread throughout the world. Savanna management of mesquite is now being promoted by many researchers and even studied by some ranchers. Due to mesquite's soil-enriching capability and its ability to provide livestock fodder and cover, savanna management of mesquite may become the preferred management scheme. Set-aside areas of mesquite forests can be allocated for timber production and eventual biomass energy usage.

Mesquite's use in solid wood products such as furniture, flooring, and wall paneling will increase. Advances in methods of sawmilling and woodworking will result in lower production costs and subsequent lower prices to the consumer, raising the demand for mesquite products. Technical improvements in small-scale veneer slicing technology will greatly increase the production of mesquite veneers and will open the door for many product applications previously not feasible for mesquite, such as large-scale production of wall paneling and furniture. Plantings of extensive mesquite timber stands with trees selected specifically for their straightness and absence of defects are currently being considered.

As demands increase for dryland planting of ornamentals, mesquite will play a greater role. Mesquite's ability to withstand long-term drought will make it more attractive than many other competing ornamental trees.

Mesquite is a unique tree resource. Its pods, leaves, wood, flowers, gum, roots, and sap all have been used by humans for thousands of years. It enriches its ecosystem through its contribution of organic matter and nitrogen. Only now are we truly realizing what a tremendous resource we have to help us in bettering our lives. Mesquite's future is bright.

The exquisite deep reddish-brown color of mesquite wood allows the artist to make wondrous wooden items such as this jewelry box crafted by Ralph Schleicher of San Antonio. (Photo © Ken E. Rogers)

Appendix 1
The Genus Prosopis *(Family Leguminosae/Fabaceae) and Its Species*

(Summarized from Burkart 1976)

Family Leguminosae/Fabaceae
Most produce their seeds in legumes or pods.

Subfamily Mimosoideae
Small flowers clustered into inflorescence.
Pinnately compound leaves with stipules.
Regular flowers with a five-part corolla.

Genus *Prosopis*
More or less fleshy pod.
Pod does not open to release the seeds when it is mature (indehiscent).
Pollen is released as single grains rather than clusters.
Forty-four species in arid and semiarid areas of North America, South America, northern Africa, and eastern Asia.

Species (scientific and common names with their geographical range)

1. *Prosopis cineraria*
   jand, ghaf, shumi (the Middle East: Saudi Arabia, Iran, Afghanistan, Pakistan, and India)

2. *Prosopis farcta* var. *farcta*
   acatin (throughout the Middle East: Algeria, Tunisia, Egypt, Turkey, Cyprus, Syria, Israel, Iran, Afghanistan, Pakistan, Transcaucasia, and Russia)

   Prosopis farcta var. *glabra*

3. *Prosopis koelziana*
   (restricted to the desert of Iran)

4. *Prosopis africana*
(central Africa: Senegal, Guinea-Bissau to Nigeria, the Cameroons, Sudan, Uganda, and Ethiopia)

5. *Prosopis strombulifera* var. *strombulifera*
retortuño, espinilla (western Argentina, northern Chile)

Prosopis strombulifera var. *ruiziana*
(Argentina)

6. *Prosopis reptans*
mastuerzo, retortuño (central Peru in Huancavelica province and central Argentina)

Prosopis reptans var. *cinerascens*
screwbean (Texas and adjacent areas of Mexico)

7. *Prosopis abbreviata*
algarrobillo espinoso (west-central Argentina)

8. *Prosopis torquata*
tintitaco, quenti (northwestern provinces of Argentina)

9. *Prosopis pubescens*
screwbean, tornillo (southwestern United States, Baja California, northern Mexico)

10. *Prosopis palmeri*
palo de hierro, palo fierro (endemic to Baja California, California)

11. *Prosopis burkartii*
(Chile in Tarapacá province)

12. *Prosopis ferox*
churqui (southern Bolivia and most northern parts of Argentina in the puna)

13. *Prosopis tamarugo*
tamarugo (northern Chile in Tarapacá province)

14. *Prosopis argentina*
algarobilla (western Argentina in the provinces of Catamarca, La Rioja, and Mendoza)

15. *Prosopis sericantha*
temoj, barba de tigre (Argentina in Gran Chaco and Monte regions)

16. *Prosopis kuntzei*
itin, palo mataco (Gran Chaco area of northern Paraguay, southern Bolivia, northern and central Argentina)

17. *Prosopis ruscifolia*
venal, chamacoco (eastern Bolivia, southern Paraguay, north-central Argentina, northeastern Brazil)

18. *Prosopis fiebrigii*
(the Chaco of Paraguay and Formosa in Argentina)

19. *Prosopis vinalillo*
vinalilla (Argentina in the Gran Chaco region and the Chaco of Paraguay)

20. *Prosopis hassleri* var. *hassleri*
algarrobo (Paraguay and Argentina in the eastern Chaco)

Prosopis hassleri var. *nigroides*

21. *Prosopis denudans* var. *denudans*
algarrobo, patagónico (endemic to southern Argentina in the Patagonia area)

Prosopis denudans var. *patagonica*
algarrobillo, espinillo

Prosopis denudans var. *stenocarpa*

22. *Prosopis ruizleali*
(restricted to western Argentina in Mendoza province)

23. *Prosopis castellanosii*
(restricted to western Argentina in the provinces of Mendoza and Neuquén)

24. *Prosopis calingastana*
cusqui (Argentina in the mountains of the province of San Juan)

25. *Prosopis humilis*
algarobilla, barba de tigre (endemic to the pampas and semi-open woodlands of central Argentina)

26. *Prosopis rojasiana*
(Paraguay in the northern Chaco)

27. *Prosopis rubriflora*
espinillo (northeastern Paraguay, Brazil in the Mato Grosso)

28. *Prosopis campestris*
algarrobillo (central Argentina in mountains of the provinces of Córdoba and San Luis)

29. *Prosopis pallida*
algarrobo, huarango (Colombia, Ecuador, Peru; introduced into Puerto Rico, the Hawaiian Islands, the Marquesas, and parts of Brazil, India, and Australia)

30. *Prosopis affinis*
nandubay, espinillo (Paraguay, eastern Argentina, north of province of Buenos Aires, Brazil southwest of Rio Grande do Sul, western Uruguay, and extreme southern Bolivia)

31. *Prosopis articulata*
mesquite, amargo (northwestern Mexico in Sonora and Baja California, and possibly Arizona)

32. *Prosopis elata*
algarrobito (Paraguay and Argentina in the Gran Chaco)

33. *Prosopis tamaulipana*
mesquite (Mexico in the states of Tamaulipas and Veracruz)

34. *Prosopis chilensis* var. *chilensis*
algarrobo de Chile, algarroba, panta (central Chile, northwestern Argentina, dry areas of Bolivia, and southern Peru)

Prosopis chilensis var. *riojana*
capesi (Argentina, La Rioja)

Prosopis chilensis var. *catamarcana*
capesi

35. *Prosopis juliflora* var. *juliflora*
mesquite, algarrobo (dry areas of Mexico [especially southern Mexico], Central America, West Indies, northern Venezuela, Colombia; introduced into Brazil)

Prosopis juliflora var. *inermis*
algarrobo, mesquite (Ecuador)

Prosopis juliflora var. *horrida*
algarrobo (northern Peru)

36. *Prosopis nigra* var. *nigra*
algarrobo negro (southern Bolivia, northern Argentina, Paraguay, and western Uruguay)

Prosopis nigra var. *ragonesei*
algarrobo amarillo (Argentina in the provinces of Santa Fe, Dept. San Justo, Dept. Vera, etc.)

Prosopis nigra var. *longispina*
algarrobillo (Argentina in the provinces of Corrientes and Eastern Chaco)

37. *Prosopis caldenia*
caldén (south-central Argentina)

38. *Prosopis laevigata* var. *laevigata*
mesquite, mezquite, algarrobo (northern Mexico's central plateau and hillsides, southern Texas, central and southern Peru, Bolivia, and northern Argentina)

Prosopis laevigata var. *andicola*
algarrobo, thako (Quechua) (southern Peru through the Bolivian Andes to the extreme northwestern corner of Argentina)

39. *Prosopis flexuosa* var. *subinermis*
algarrobo, algarrobo dulce or negro (western Argentina in the Monte Desert)

40. *Prosopis glandulosa* var. *glandulosa*
honey mesquite, mesquite (Texas, New Mexico, eastern Arizona, Oklahoma, Nevada, and Utah, northeastern Mexico; cultivated in Puerto Rico and parts of Asia and Australia)

Prosopis glandulosa var. *torreyana*
honey mesquite (eastern Arizona, New Mexico, western Texas, California, northern Mexico; introduced into Saudi Arabia, Pakistan, India, Burma, southern and southwestern Africa)

Prosopis glandulosa var. *prostrata*
running mesquite, mesquite rastrero (Texas, Mexico in Tamaulipas)

41. *Prosopis alpataco*
alpataco (west-central Argentina in the central and southern Monte Desert)

42. *Prosopis alba* var. *alba*
algarrobo blanco, igope or ibope-para (plains of subtropical Argentina to Uruguay, Paraguay, southern Bolivia to Peru)

Prosopis alba var. *panta*
algarrobo panta, algarrobo impanta (northwestern Argentina and southern Bolivia, eastern Gran Chaco, Paraguay)

43. *Prosopis velutina*
velvet mesquite (southern Arizona and adjacent California, into Mexico)

44. *Prosopis pugionata*
algarrobo de las salinas, alpataco (central and western Argentina in the provinces of Córdoba, La Rioja, Catamarca, San Juan, and San Luis)

Appendix 2
Sources of Information

Ken E. Rogers
P. O. Box 9009
College Station, TX 77842
Tele: (409) 764-2936
Fax: (503) 961-1570
Email: krogers@tca.net

Department of Rangeland Ecology and Management
Texas A&M University
College Station, TX 77845-2126
Tele: (409) 845-0302

Texas Forest Service
Forest Products Laboratory
P.O. Box 310
Lufkin, TX 75901
Tele: (409) 639-8180
Fax: (409) 639-8185
Email: krogers@tca.net
(The laboratory has extensive information on mesquite wood, wood drying, sawmilling, wood processing, and wood in-service usage and acts as a clearinghouse for information on mesquite.)

Los Amigos del Mesquite
Texas A&M University at Kingsville
Kingsville, TX 78363

Robert Hensarling
The Texas Mesquite Association
Hwy 90 East
Uvalde, TX 78801

Robert Ohm
Caesar Kleberg Wildlife Research Institute
Texas A&M University at Kingsville
Kingsville, TX 78363
(Operates Listserve on the Internet entitled PROSOPIS.)

USDA, Agricultural Research Service
P.O. Box 748
Temple, TX 76503

Brazos Valley Wood Products
#1 Mesquite Tree Lane
Marlin, TX 76661-2059
Tele: (254) 883-5056
(Information on sources of mesquite cooking woods.)

References and Further Reading

The following selected works provide information on the mesquite, its history, and its place in the southwestern United States and the world. In addition, a wealth of information can readily be obtained via the World Wide Web.

Adams, Don. 1968. *Chemical Analysis of Mesquite Wood.* Texas Forest Service Pamphlet No. 5. Forest Products Laboratory, Lufkin.

Adams, Faye Carr. 1948. Mesquite. In *Sweet Is the Homing Hour*, p. 52. Kaleidograph Press, Dallas, Texas.

———. 1968. Where Longhorn Bones Lie Bleached. In *More Than a Loaf*, pp. 46–47. Naylor Press, San Antonio, Texas.

Ahmed, A. E. H. 1986. Some Aspects of Dry Land Afforestation in the Sudan with Special Reference to *Acacia tortilis* (Forsk.) Hayne, *A. senegal* Willd. and *Prosopis chilensis* (Molina) Stuntz. *Forest Ecology and Management* 16: 209–221.

Allred, B. W. 1949. Distribution and Control of Several Woody Plants in Texas and Oklahoma. *Journal of Range Management* 2: 17–19.

Almanza, S. G., and E. G. Moya. 1986. The Uses of Mesquite (*Prosopis* spp.) in the Highlands of San Luis Potosí, Mexico. *Forest Ecology and Management* 16 (1986): 49–56.

Andres, C., ed. 1985. Mesquite Smoke Flavoring Becoming National Phenomenon. *Food Processing* 46, no. 2: 46.

Ansley, R. James, and J. F. Cadenhead III. 1996. Mesquite Savanna: A Brush Management Option. *Cattleman* 83: 10–12.

Archer, Steve. 1989. Have Southern Texas Savannas Been Converted to Woodlands in Recent History? *American Naturalist* 134, no. 4 (October): 545–561.

———. 1994. Woody Plant Encroachment into Southwestern Grasslands and Savannas: Rates, Patterns and Proximate Causes. In *Ecological Implications of Livestock Herbivory in the West*, ed. M. Vavra, W. A. Laycock, and R. D. Pieper, pp. 13–68. Society for Range Management, Denver.

———. 1995. Tree-Grass Dynamics in a *Prosopis*-Thornscrub Savanna Parkland: Reconstructing the Past and Predicting the Future. *Ecoscience* 2: 83–99.

Archer, Steve, M. Garrett, and J. K. Detling. 1987. Rates of Vegetation Change Associated with Prairie Dog (*Cynomys ludovicianus*) Grazing in North American Mixed-Grass Prairie. *Vegetatio* 72: 159–166.

Archer, Steve, C. J. Scifres, C. R. Bassha, and R. Maggio. 1988. Autogenic Succession in Subtropical Savanna: Conversion of Grassland to Thornland. *Ecological Monographs* 58: 111–127.

Aschenbach, J. 1985. Mesquite—A Pest with Good Taste. *National Geographic* News Service. August 7.

Australian Quarantine and Inspection Services (AQIS). 1996. (Online) Mesquites. http://www.dpie.gov.au/aqis/homepage/public/industry/mesquite.html.

Bailey, A. W. 1976. Nitrogen Fixation in Honey Mesquite Seedlings. *Journal of Range Management* 29, no. 6: 479–481.

Baird, L. M., R. A. Virginia, and B. D. Webster. 1985. Development of Root Nodules in a Woody Legume, *Prosopis glandulosa* Torr. *Botanical Gazette* 146: 39–43.

Bartlett, J. R. 1965. Personal Narrative of Explorations and Incidents in Texas, New Mexico, and California, Sonora, and Chihuahua. 1854. 2 vols. Reprint. Rio Grande Press, Chicago.

Beasom, S. L. 1988. Importance of South Texas Brush, Including Mesquite, for Wildlife Habitat. In *Los Amigos del Mesquite Annual Meeting Proceedings* (September): 4–6.

Bell, J. G. 1932. A Log of the Texas-California Cattle Trail, 1854. *Southwestern Historical Quarterly* 35: 208–237, 290–316.

Benson, L. 1941. The Mesquites and Screw-Beans of the United States. *American Journal of Botany* 28(11): 748–754.

Berlandier, J. L. 1969. *The Indians of Texas in 1830*. Ed. J. L. Ewers. Smithsonian Institution Press, Washington, D.C.

Bogusch, E. R. 1950. A Bibliography on Mesquite. *Texas Journal of Science* 4 (December): 528–538.

———. 1951. Climatic Limits Affecting Distribution of Mesquite (*Prosopis juliflora*) in Texas. *Texas Journal of Science* 4 (December): 554–558.

Bracht, Viktor. 1931. *Texas in 1848*. Naylor Printing Company, San Antonio.

Britton, N. L. 1884. The Range of *Phoradendron*. *Bulletin of the Torrey Botanical Club* 11: 76.

Brown, J. R. 1987. Factors Regulating the Ingress and Establishment of a Woody Plant (*Prosopis glandulosa*) in Perennial Grasslands. Ph.D. thesis. Texas A&M University, College Station.

Buffington, L. C., and C. H. Herbel. 1965. Vegetational Changes on a Semidesert Grassland Range from 1858–1963. *Ecological Monographs* 35, no. 2: 139–164.

Burkart, Arturo. 1976. A Monograph of the Genus *Prosopis* (Leguminosae Subfam. Mimosoideae). *Journal of the Arnold Arboretum* 57: 219–255, 458–530.

Carman, N. J., and T. J. Mabry. 1975. Disjunction of *Prosopis reptans* and the Origin of the North American Populations. *Biochemical Systematics* 3: 19–23.

Clopper, J. C. 1828. Journal and Book of Memoranda for 1928. *Southwestern Historical Quarterly* 13, no. 1: 44–80.

Coghlan, A. 1995. Mistletoe's Kiss of Death Revealed. *New Scientist* 4: 21.

Commissioner of Agriculture. 1871. Food Products of the North American Indians. In *Report of the Commissioner of Agriculture for the Year 1870*, 410–412. Government Printing Office, Washington, D.C.

Cook, O. F. 1908. Change of Vegetation on the South Texas Prairies. Circ. No. 14. USDA Bureau of Plant Industries, Temple, Texas.

Cordo, H. A., and C. J. DeLoach. 1987. *Insects That Attack Mesquite (*Prosopis *spp.) in Argentina and Paraguay*. USDA Agr. Res. Ser. ARS-62, Temple, Texas. May. 32 pp.

Cornejo-Oviedo, E. H. 1989. Managing Immature and Mature Mesquite (*Prosopis glandulosa* var. *glandulosa*) Stands for Hardwood Lumber Production and Pasture Improvement. M.S. thesis. Texas A&I University, Kingsville.

Cornejo-Oviedo, E. H., S. Gronski, and P. Felker. 1992. Mature Mesquite (*Prosopis glandulosa* var. *glandulosa*) Stand Description and Preliminary Effects of Understory Removal and Fertilization on Growth. *Journal of Arid Environments* 22: 339–351.

Craig, Jean. 1997. How to Smoke and Barbeque with Mesquite. Letter to Author. Brazos Valley Wood Products, Marlin, Texas.

———. 1998. How to Make Mesquite Jelly. Letter to Author. Brazos Valley Wood Products, Marlin, Texas.

Cuda, J. P., C. J. DeLoach, and T. O. Robbins. 1990. Population Dynamics of *Melipotis indomita* (Lepidoptera: Noctuidae), an Indigenous Natural Enemy of Mesquite, *Prosopis* spp. *Environmental Entomology* 19, no. 2: 415–422.

Dahl, B. E. 1982. Mesquite as a Rangeland Plant. In *Mesquite Utilization Symposium*, pp. A1–A20. Texas Tech University, Lubbock.

Davenport, H., and J. K. Wells. 1919. The First Europeans in Texas, 1528–1536. *Southwestern Historical Quarterly* 22, no. 3: 205–228.

Davidson, B. R., and H. F. Davidson. 1992. *Legumes: The Australian Experience*. Research Studies Press, Ltd., Taunton, Somerset, England.

Deloach, C. J. 1985. Conflicts of Interest over Beneficial and Undesirable Aspects of Mesquite (*Prosopis* spp.) in the United States as Related to Biological Control. In *Proceedings of the VIth International Symposium on the Biological Control of Weeds, 19–25 August 1984, Vancouver, Canada*, ed. E. S. Delfosse, Agric. Can., pp. 301–340.

Del Valle, F. R., E. Marco, R. Becker, and R. M. Saunders. 1988a. Development of Products Containing Mesquite *Prosopis* (spp.) Pod Flour and Their Nutritional and Organoleptic Evaluation. *Journal of Food Processing and Preservation* 13: 447–456.

———. 1988b. Evaluation of an Industrial Process for Producing Protein Enriched Mesquite Pod (*Prosopis* species) Flour. *Journal of Food Processing and Preservation* 12:179–185.

Dobie, J. F. 1941a. Mesquite. *Arizona Highways* 11: 4–7, 44, 45.

———. 1941b. Mesquite: The Characteristic Growth of the Southwest. In My Texas Column, *Dallas Morning News*, February 9, p. 12, and February 16, p. 8.

———. 1943. The Conquering Mesquite. *Natural History* 51 (May): 208–217.

Dutton, R. W., ed. 1992. Prosopis *Species: Aspects of Their Value, Research, and Development*. Proceedings, *Prosopis* Symposium. Centre for Overseas Research and Development (CORD), University of Durham, UK, July 27–31. 320 pp.

Earl, P. R. 1958. *Prosopis* as a Subtropical Crop in Mexico. *International Tree Crops Journal* 3: 185–186.

El Youssouf, Moulay-Mustapha. 1972. Factors Influencing Recruitment of Honey Mesquite (*Prosopis glandulosa* var. *glandulosa*) in a

Savanna Woodland, Texas. Ph.D. thesis. Texas A&M University, College Station.

Esbenshade, H. W. 1980. Kiawe (*Prosopis pallida*): A Tree in Hawaii. *International Tree Crops Journal* 1, no. 213: 125–130.

Fagg, C. W., and J. L. Stewart. 1994. The Value of *Acacia* and *Prosopis* in Arid and Semi-arid Environments. *Journal of Arid Environments* 27: 3–25.

Felger, R. S. 1977. Mesquite in Indian Cultures of Southwestern North America. In *Mesquite*, by B. B. Simpson, Chapter 8, pp. 150–176. Dowden, Hutchinson, and Ross, Inc., Stroudsburg, Penn.

Felker, P. 1979. Mesquite: An All-Purpose Leguminous Arid Land Tree. In *New Agricultural Crops*, ed. G. A. Ritchie, pp. 89–132. Selected Symposium No. 38. American Association for the Advancement of Science (AAAS). Westview Press, Boulder, Colo.

Felker, P., and P. R. Clark. 1980. Nitrogen Fixation (Acetylene Reduction) and Cross Inoculation in 12 *Prosopis* (Mesquite) Species. *Plant and Soil* 57: 177–186.

Felker, P., P. R. Clark, A. E. Laag, and P. F. Pratt. 1981. Salinity Tolerance of the Tree Legumes: Mesquite (*Prosopis glandulosa* var. *torreyana*, *P. velutina*, and *P. articulata*), Algarrobo (*P. chilensis*), Kiawe (*P. pallida*), and Tamarugo (*P. tamarugo*) Grown in Sand Culture on Nitrogen-Free Media. *Plant and Soil* 61: 311–317.

Felker, P., J. Meyer, and S. Gronski. 1986. *Managing Mesquite for Lumber, Cattle, and Wildlife*. Center for Semi-Arid Forest Resources, Caesar Kleberg Wildlife Research Institute, Texas A&M University at Kingsville.

———. 1988. Application of Self-Thinning in Mesquite to Range Management and Lumber Production. *Forest Ecology and Management* 31: 225–232.

Felker, P., and J. Moss, eds. 1996. Prosopis: *Semiarid Fuelwood and Forage Tree Building Consensus for the Disenfranchised, a Workshop 13–15 March, 1996, Texas A&M—Kingsville*. 400 pp.

Felker, P., and S. Roberson. 1982. *Mesquite Woodworking*. Caesar Kleberg Wildlife Research Institute, Kingsville, Texas.

Forbes, R. H. 1895. *The Mesquite Tree*. Bulletin No. 13. Arizona Agricultural Experiment Station, Tucson. 25 pp.

Foster, J. H. 1917. General Survey of Texas Woodlands, Including a

Study of the Commercial Possibilities of Mesquite. *Bulletin of the Agr. and Mech. College of Texas* 3, no. 9: 40–46.

Francis, Francis, Jr. 1887. *Saddle and Mocassin* [*sic*]. Chapman, and Hall, Ltd., London. 322 pp.

Friend, L. M., ed. 1967. *M. K. Kellogg's Texas Journal 1872*. University of Texas Press, Austin.

Fuchs, T. W., D. N. Ueckert, and B. M. Drees. 1990. (Online) Desert Termites—UC-16. Texas Agricultural Extension Service, Texas A&M University, College Station. Http://entowww.tamu.edu/extension/bulletins/uc/uc-016.html.

Gard, W. 1954. Mesquite Jungles of Texas. *Think*. (February): 5–7.

Gill, H. S. 1986. *Prosopis juliflora* Excels in Extremely Alkaline Soils. Paper presented at Annual Meeting of Los Amigos del Mesquite, September 13. Indian Council of Agricultural Research, New Delhi.

Gill, L. S., and F. G. Hawksworth. 1961. *The Mistletoes: A Literature Review*. Techn. Bulletin No. 1242. USDA, Washington D.C.

Green, A. C. 1969. Mesquite and Mountain Cedar. *Southwest Review* 54, no. 3: 314–320.

Greenwood, C., and P. Morey. 1979. Gumnosis in Honey Mesquite. *Botanical Gazette* 140, no. 1: 32–38.

Gregg, Josiah. 1954. *Commerce of the Prairies*. Ed. M. L. Moorhead. University of Oklahoma Press, Norman.

Grimes, Frank. 1928. The Old Mesquites Ain't Out. *Abilene Reporter-News*, March 28.

Gronski, Steven J. 1987. The Management of Mature Stands of Mesquite (*Prosopis glandulosa* var. *glandulosa*) for Timber Production. M.S. thesis. Texas A&I University, Kingsville.

Gupta, R. K., and G. S. Balara. 1972. Comparative Studies on the Germination, Growth, and Seedling Biomass of Two Promising Exotics in the Rajasthar Desert. *Indian Forester* 98:280–285.

Habit, M. A. 1981. Prosopis tamarugo: *Fodder Tree for Arid Zones*. FAO Plant Production and Protection Papers, 25. United Nations, Rome.

Hacker, J. B. 1995. *A Guide to Herbaceous and Shrub Legumes of Queensland*. University of Queensland Press, St. Lucia.

Haller, J. M. 1981. The Tree That Defies Nails. *American Forests* (March): 19+.

Hanselka, W. 1998. Nitrogen, Phosphorus, and Carbon Storage by Mesquite. Paper presented at the Annual Meeting of Los Amigos del Mesquite, September 25, Corpus Christi, Texas.

Hatch, S. L., and J. Pluhar. *Texas Range Plants.* Texas A&M University Press, College Station.

Havard, V. 1884. The Mezquit. *American Naturalist* 18, no. 5 (May): 451–460.

———. 1895. Food Plants of the North American Indians. *Bulletin of the Torrey Botanical Club* 23, no. 3: 98–123.

———. 1896. Drink Plants of the North American Indians. *Bulletin of the Torrey Botanical Club* 23, no. 2: 33–45.

Hellden, V. 1988. Desertification Monitoring: Is the Desert Encroaching? *Desertification Control Bulletin* 17: 8–12.

House, B. 1950. Mesquite. In *Texas Rhythm and Other Poems,* 46–47. Naylor Press, San Antonio.

Hughes, C. E., and B. T. Styles. 1987. The Benefits and Potential Risks of Woody Legume Introductions. *International Tree Crop Journal* 4: 209–248.

Jenkins, M. B., R. A. Virginia, and W. M. Jarrell. 1989. Ecology of Fast Grown and Slow Grown Mesquite Nodulating Rhizobia in Chihuahuan and Sonoran Desert Ecosystems. *Soil Science Society Annual Journal* 53: 543–549.

Johnson, H. B., and H. S. Mayeux, Jr. 1990. *Prosopis glandulosa* and the Nitrogen Balance of Rangelands: Extent and Occurrence of Nodulation. *Oecologia* 84: 176–185.

Johnston, M. C. 1962. The North American Mesquites. *Prosopis* Section *Algarobia* (Leguminosae). *Brittonia* 14 (January): 72–90.

———. 1963. Past and Present Grasslands of Southern Texas and Northeastern Mexico. *Ecology* 44, no. 3: 456–466.

Judd, C. S. 1916. The First Algaroba and Royal Palm in Hawaii. *Hawaiian Forester and Agriculturist* 13: 330–335.

———. 1920. Original Algaroba Tree Gone. *Hawaiian Forester and Agriculturist* 17, no. 9: 308–309.

Kassas, M. 1995. Desertification: A General Review. *Journal of Arid Environments* 30: 115–128.

Kendall, G. W. 1844. *Narrative of the Texas Santa Fe Expedition.* 2 vols. Harper and Brothers, New York.

Kreder, V. 1988. Mesquite Utilization in the Food Flavoring Industry. In *Los Amigos del Mesquite Annual Meeting Proceedings.* (September): 18–20.

Lanier, Sidney. 1913. The Texas Trail in the 70's. *Outlook* (November 15): 582–585.

Lee, Jim, ed. 1986. *Mesquite—Its Roots Are Deep in the Heart of Texas.* Hummer Press, Reagan Wells, Texas. 115 pp.

Major Plant Weed and Biological Control Agents. 1998. (Online) In Agriculture—Environmental Conditions & Pressures. NSW Environment Protection Authority, Australia. Http://www.epa.nsw.au/soe/95/23_2t1.htm.

Marmillon, E. 1986. Management of Algarrobo in the Semi-arid Region of Argentina. *Forest Ecology and Management* 16 (1986): 33–40.

Marshall, E. D. 1945. Utilization of Mesquite. Texas Forest Research Note No. 3. Texas Forest Products Laboratory, Lufkin. 14 pp.

McClintock, W. A. 1930. Journal of a Trip through Texas and Northern Mexico in 1846–1847. *Southwestern Historical Quarterly* 34: 20–36, 141–158, 231–256.

McLauchlan, R. A., A. Conkey, G. Scherer, and P. Felker. 1994. Development of a Flail Harvester for Small Diameter Brushland Coppiced Trees to Produce Energy/Chemical Feedstock. Paper presented at the Mechanization in Short Rotation, Intensive Culture Forestry Conference, March 1–3, Mobile, Ala.

Mesquite. 1996. *New Handbook of Texas.* Texas State Historical Association, Austin.

The Miracle Trees That Drank the Water. 1997. (Online) Electronic Mail & Guardian, PANA/Misa, November 6. Http://196.2.18.61/mg/news/97nov1/6nov-sudan.html.

Moore, Harry B. 1979. *Wood Inhabiting Insects in Houses: Their Identification, Biology, Prevention, and Control.* USDA, Forest Service, and the U.S. Dept. of Housing and Urban Development, Washington, D.C. 133 pp.

Nelson, R. E., and P. R. Wheeler. 1963. Forest Resources of Hawaii—1961. USDA Forest Service, Pac. S.W. Forest Range Experiment Station and Hawaii Department of Land and Natural Resources, Division of Forestry, Berkeley and Honolulu, Hawaii. 48 pp.

Newcomb, W. W., Jr. 1961. *The Indians of Texas: From Prehistoric to Modern Times.* University of Texas Press, Austin.

Nilsen, E. T., P. W. Rundel, and M. R. Shariffi. 1981. Summer Water Relations of the Desert Phreatophyte *Prosopis glandulosa* in the Sonoran Desert of Southern California. *Oecologia* 50: 271–276.

Nimbkar, B. V., N. Nimbkar, and N. Zende. 1986. Desertification of Western Maharashtra: Causes and Possible Solutions. I. Comparative Growth of Eight Tree Species. *Forest Ecology and Management* 16: 243–251.

Nixon, K. C., and C. A. Todzia. 1985. Within-Population, Within-Host Species, and Within-Host Tree Sex Ratios in Mistletoe (*Phoradendron tomentosum*) in Central Texas. *American Midland Naturalist* 114, no. 2: 304–310.

Noach, H. M. 1997. Welcome to Mesquiteville! Love It or Curse It, Scrappy Tree Is Part of Our History and Lives. *Wichita Falls Times Record News*, April 20.

Olsson, L. 1985. *An Integrated Study of Desertification*. Lund Studies in Geography Ser. C. General and Mathematical Geography (13). Lund, Sweden. 170 pp.

Parker, R. D. 1987. *Insect Pests on Ornamental Mesquites and Methods of Their Control*. Texas Agricultural Extension Services, Corpus Christi. 17 pp.

Pattie, James Ohio. 1831. *The Personal Narrative of James O. Pattie of Kentucky during an Expedition from St. Louis, through the Vast Regions between That Place and the Pacific Ocean*. E. H. Flint Co., Cincinnati, Ohio. 300 pp.

Plant Protection and Quarantine. USDA Animal and Plant Health Inspection Service (Aphis). 1976. *Part 36—Noxious Weed Regulations. Authority: 7 U.S.C. 2803 and 2809; 7CRF2.17,2.51, and 371.2(c)*. Riverdale, Md. Http://www.aphis.usda.gov/ppq/ss/360regs.html.

Refugia for Biological Diversity in Australia—Management Issues. 1996. (Online) Department of the Environments, Sport, and Territories. Http://environment.gov.au/life/general_info/biodivser_4/biol6.html.

Researchers Study Brush's Effects on W. Texas Water. 1997. *Dallas Morning News*, January 1, pp. 13, 16.

Rogers, Ken E. 1984. *Lumber and Clear Cutting Recovery from Mesquite (*Prosopis *spp.) Logs*. Pub. No. 135. Texas Forest Service, Lufkin.

———. 1986. *The Wood Properties of Mesquite (*Prosopis glandulosa *var:* glandulosa*): Its Basic Properties and Variability*. Pub. No. 140. Texas Forest Service, Lufkin.

———. 1989. Mesquite Utilization. *Mesquite Messenger* 6, no. 2 (Spring): 8–10.

———. 1990a. Mesquite: The Wonderful, Wondrous Wood. Marketing Brochure, Texas Forest Service, Lufkin. (Available from the Texas Forest Products Laboratory.)

———. 1990b. Methods to Kill Wood Borers in Mesquite Lumber. Unpublished report. (Available from the Texas Forest Products Laboratory.)

———. 1993. Dry Kiln Schedules for Mesquite Lumber. Unpublished report. (Available from the Texas Forest Products Laboratory.)

———. 1997. Mesquite—from Pest to Fine Woodworking. *Australian Woodworker* 71 (February): 90.

Rundel, P. W., E. T. Nilsen, M. R. Sharifi, R. A. Virginia, W. M. Jarrell, D. H. Kohl, and G. B. Sherarer. 1982. Seasonal Dynamics of Nitrogen Cycling for a *Prosopis* Woodland in the Sonora Desert. *Plant and Soil* 67: 343–353.

Sargent, C. S. 1891. *The Silva of North America*. Vol. 3. Houghton Mifflin, at the Riverside Press, Boston.

Scanlan, J. C., and S. Archer. 1991. Simulated Dynamics of Succession in a North American Subtropical *Prosopis* Savanna. *Journal of Vegetation Science* 2: 625–634.

Schmutz, E. M. 1976. Successional Classification of Plants on a Desert Grassland Site in Arizona. *Journal of Range Management* 29, no. 6: 476–478.

Schuster, J. L. 1976. *Literature on the Mesquite (*Prosopis *L.) of North America: An Annotated Bibliography*. Special Report No. 26. Texas Tech University, Lubbock.

Scifres, C. J. 1980. *Brush Management: Principles and Practices for Texas and the Southwest*. Texas A&M University Press, College Station.

Scifres, C. J., and W. T. Hamilton. 1993. *Prescribed Burning for Brushland Management: The South Texas Example*. Texas A&M University Press, College Station.

Scifres, C. J., W. T. Hamilton, J. R. Conner, J. M. Inglis, G. A. Rasmussen, R. O. Smith, J. W. Stuth, and T. G. Welch. 1985. *Integrated Brush Management Systems for South Texas: Development and Implementation*. Texas Agricultural Experiment Station, College Station.

Scott, J. 1996. Some Trees Worsen Texas' Water Situation. *Dallas Morning News*, Sunday, June 30.

Shutler, M. E. 1958. Disease and Curing in a Yaqui Community. In *Ethnic Medicines in the Southwest*, ed. E. H. Spicer, pp. 169–203. University of Arizona Press, Tucson.

Simpson, B. B., ed. 1977. *Mesquite: Its Biology in Two Desert Scrub Ecosystems.* Dowden, Hutchinson, and Ross, Inc., Stroudsburg, Pa. 247 pp.

Skolmen, R. G. 1981. *Prosopis pallida.* Unpublished Silvics handbook draft. July. USDA, Forest Service. Institute of Pacific Islands Forestry, Honolulu.

Smith, B. 1871. *Relation of Alvar Núñez Cabeza de Vaca, Translated from the Spanish.* University Microfilms, Ann Arbor.

Smither, Harriet, ed. 1927. *The Papers of Mirabeau Buonaparte Lamar.* Vols. 5 and 6. Pemberton Press, Austin, Texas.

Soil Conservation Service. 1987. *Texas Brush Inventory.* USDA, Washington, D.C. (now National Resource Conservation Service).

Soltes, E. J., ed. 1977. *Proceedings, Mesquite Utilization Conference.* Department of Forest Science, Research Note 4. Texas A&M University, College Station.

Srivastava, J. P., and J. C. Hetherington. 1991. Khejri (*Prosopis cineraria*): A Tree for the Arid and Semi-arid Zones of Rajasthan. *International Tree Crops Journal* 7: 1–16.

Swenson, J. D. 1984. A Cache of Mesquite Beans from the Mecca Hills, Salton Basin, California. *Journal of California and Great Basin Anthropology* 6, no. 2: 246–252.

Taylor, H. C., Jr. 1960. Archeological Notes on the Route of Cabeza de Vaca. *Bulletin of the Texas Archeological Society* 31: 273–290.

Teague, R., R. Borchardt, J. Ansley, B. Pinchak, J. Cox, J. Foy, and J. McGrann. 1997. Sustainable Management Strategies for Mesquite Rangeland: The Waggoner Kite Project. *Rangelands* 19, no. 5: 4–8.

Texas Agricultural Experiment Station. 1973. *Mesquite.* Research Monograph No. 1. College Station. 80 pp.

Texas Historical Association. 1910. J. C. Clopper's Journal and Book of Memoranda for 1828: The Province of Texas. *Southwestern Historical Quarterly* 13: 44–80.

Texas Tech University. 1982. *Mesquite Utilization, 1982: Papers Pre-*

sented at the Symposium on Mesquite Utilization, Texas Tech University, Lubbock, Texas, 79409, October 29 and 30, 1982. College of Agricultural Sciences, Lubbock.

Thomas, G. W., and R. E. Sosebee. 1978. Water Relations of Honey Mesquite. In *Proceedings of the First International Rangeland Congress*, ed. D. N. Hyder. Society for Range Management, Denver. 68 pp.

Turner, B. L. 1959. *The Legumes of Texas*. University of Texas Press, Austin. 250 pp.

Ulich, W. C. 1983. *Development of a Biomass Combine*. Rept. No. T-3-103. Texas Tech University, Lubbock.

United Nations. 1992. *Managing Fragile Ecosystems: Combating Desertification and Drought, Chapter 12 of Agenda 21*. United Nations, New York.

University of Hawaii. 1934. *Noxious Plants of the Hawaiian Ranges*. Extension Bulletin No. 62. Manoa. 23 pp.

United States Department of Agriculture (USDA). Bureau of Forestry. 1904. *Forests of the Hawaiian Islands*. Research Bulletin 48. Washington, D.C. 10 pp.

Vines, R. A. 1976. *Trees, Shrubs, and Woody Vines of the Southwest*. University of Texas Press, Austin.

Virginia, R. A. 1986. Soil Development under Legume Tree Canopies. *Forest Ecology and Management* 16: 69–79.

Watson, Shelley. 1984. Mesquite: For the Grill That Has Everything. *Restaurants and Institutions* 94: 181.

Weiner, H. 1995. A Ranch near Henrietta Clears a Path for Natural Brush-Control Work with Camels in the Country. *Fort Worth Star-Telegram*, June 14.

Welch, T. G. 1991. *Suggestions for Chemical Weed and Brush Control on Rangeland*. Texas Agricultural Extension Service, Department of Rangeland Ecology and Management. Rpt. B-1466. Texas A&M University, College Station.

Weldon, Dewayne. 1986. Exceptional Physical Properties of Texas Mesquite Wood. *Forest Ecology and Management* 16: 149–153.

Whitaker, Bill. 1997. Abilene Man Knows Beans about Mesquite. *Abilene Reporter-News*, September 27.

Wiley, A. T. 1977. Mesquite—A Possible Source of Energy. *Forest Products Journal* 27, no. 7: 48–51.

Wilson, S. 1984. Mesquite, the Forgotten Manna of the Southwest. *Great Plains Historical Journal* 23: 82–105.

Wiltzin, J. F., S. Archer, and R. K. Heitschmidt. 1997. Small Mammal Regulation of Vegetation Structure in a Temperate Savanna. *Ecology* 78: 751–763.

Wright, C. C. 1965. The Mesquite Tree: From Nature's Boon to Aggressive Invader. *Southwestern Historical Quarterly* 69: 38–43.

Yoakum, Henderson K. 1855. *History of Texas from Its First Settlement in 1685 to Its Annexation to the United States in 1846.* 2 vols. Redfield, New York.

Zelada, L. G. 1986. The Influence of the Productivity of *Prosopis tamaruga* on Livestock Production in the Pampa de Tamarugal—A Review. *Forest Ecology and Management* 16: 15–31.

Zollner, D. 1986. Sand Dune Stabilization in Central Somalia. *Forest Ecology and Management* 16: 223–232.

Index